WITHDRAWN

THE PREVENTION
AND CONTROL
OF DELINQUENCY

THE AUTHOR

Robert M. MacIver is a former President and Chancellor of the New School for Social Research and the founder of its Center for New York City Affairs.

One of the most influential figures in modern sociology, he has held major appointments at Columbia University and the University of Toronto and has been the recipient of eight honorary doctorates. Dr. MacIver is a Fellow of the American Academy of Arts and Sciences, the British Academy, the World Academy of Arts and Science, and the American Philosophical Society, as well as a member of various learned societies. Among his many books are *Community, a Sociological Study; The Modern State; The Web of Government; Society, an Introductory Analysis;* and *Social Causation.*

Robert M. MacIver

THE PREVENTION
AND CONTROL
OF DELINQUENCY

Atherton Press

New York · 1967

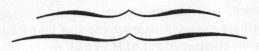

Preface

Having been engaged for nearly six years in a close-up study of the agencies in New York City concerned with juvenile delinquency—police, courts, departments of correction, health, welfare, supervising bodies including the Youth Board, detention houses, public and private custodial institutions, settlements, special schools and educational programs, charitable organizations, research agencies—I came to the conclusion that much of this great system of services was ineffectual in coping with a growing and perplexing problem. There were some admirable "residential treatment centers," some well-organized departments, and some devoted workers, but there was a lack of overall strategy, a failure to get down to the roots of the problem. This was broadly the conclusion arrived at by my research colleagues, too, while I was directing the City of New York Juvenile Delinquency Research Project. We made a considerable number of specific recommendations, some of which were acted upon. On the whole there have been some welcome developments recently, not only in the area we studied but also in other areas across the country. There is still, however, a great need for the application of the knowledge we now possess as a guide to an inclusive strategy of delinquency control.

I was therefore happy to welcome the opportunity presented by a grant from the National Institute of Mental Health to undertake a broader study, seeking to provide a perspective on the problem as a whole, the conditions under which delinquency occurs more frequently and less frequently, the groups most affected by it, the causes to which the higher and lower incidence are attributed, and the consequent strategy that research and experience have shown to be most effective in dealing with it. I appreciate the courtesy of N.I.M.H., which readily permitted me to postpone my work and finish it in installments when important obligations of another kind made it difficult or impossible for me to carry on as I had originally agreed. My grateful acknowledgment is also owed Miss Jeanette Gevov, who had been a researcher during my work for New York City and who did effective work as my assistant by collecting, organizing, and preparing reports on recent developments across the country in the areas covered in Part Three of this study.

I have not sought to give an exhaustive or detailed account of the numerous developments discussed in Part Three. This book is intended to state a problem and its setting so as to derive from this analysis directions for effective action in the various areas and various stages and types of delinquent behavior. It gives a concrete description of the more important devices and experiments that are now being developed and practiced. It should therefore be serviceable to organizational leaders and workers, to educators and planners active in this field, and generally to students in the social sciences.

Robert M. MacIver

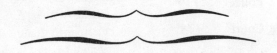

Contents

Part One

THE ASSOCIATED

CONDITIONS

1

The Statistical Picture

In this study we offer a perspective on juvenile delinquency as it has developed in this country and seek to show how our present knowledge bears on the question of its prevention and control. There is an extensive literature on the subject, the most significant contributions being scattered through various learned and professional journals and government reports. Many variant or conflicting explanations are put forward to account for the continuing increase in the amount of delinquency as measured by statistical indices, and more than a few divergent proposals are made as an answer to the problem. Many agencies, both public and private, are directing their energies and contributing considerable sums of money to remedial methods. Nevertheless, there are no significant indications of any general improvement. In this writer's experience, much of the official treatment of delinquents is still little affected by the findings of the research that has been devoted to the subject.

The statistical record is certainly alarming. Practically every year it shows a further increase in the proportion of delinquency. In the United States between 1948 and 1957 juvenile court cases more than doubled, whereas the youth population ten through seventeen years increased during the period by only 27 per cent. Between 1940 and 1961 court cases increased 400 per cent. The phenomenon is by no means peculiar to the United States. In Britain in 1962 delinquency was statistically twice as high for boys and three times as high for girls as it was before the First World War.[1] Western Germany reports an increase of 39.2 per cent in "convicted juveniles" fourteen to eighteen years old between 1951 and 1957, Eastern Germany an increase of juvenile offenses of 96.3 per cent for the same period.[2] Austria reports an increase of 68 per cent in "convicted juveniles" fourteen to eighteen years old between 1951 and 1956. Finland shows an increase of 61.7 per cent in its juvenile offenders fifteen to seventeen years old. Sweden reports between 1950 and 1956 an increase of 210 per cent of juveniles under fifteen years "suspected of criminal behavior." Switzerland shows an increase in the various cantons.

Public concern has been aroused particularly by the headlines reporting gang "rumbles," stabbings, shootings, and vandalism. It is impossible to derive any precise measurement of the volume of delinquency or of the actual increase that may have occurred. The various indices we employ—police arrests, court appearances, juvenile delinquency adjudications, institutional commitments—are all affected by changes in socioeconomic conditions, by the number of delinquency petitions from non-police sources, by the available space in the institutions to which delinquents are committed, by changes in methods of reporting cases, by changes in the number and in the character of juvenile courts, by developments in the voluntary welfare agencies, and even by the degree of public concern over the amount of juvenile delinquency.

The statistics are nevertheless significant as probable indicators of a trend. If arrests of juveniles in New York City more than tripled between 1950 and 1959, it is reasonable to conclude that some of the increase in the amount of delinquency is real, not merely statistical. A Children's Bureau report calculates that as many as 12 per cent of all juveniles have been cited at least once for court appearance between their tenth and seventeenth birthdays. And we must bear in mind that much delinquent behavior escapes the notice of the authorities.[3]

A clear indication that the volume of delinquency has definitely increased over recent years is that really serious offenses, assaults on the person, shootings, stabbings, and other felonies, have grown roughly in proportion to the number of minor offenses. Such offenses are less likely to be unreported, negotiated out of court, or ignored because of influence or otherwise. We must therefore conclude that conditions in our society, conditions bearing especially on the morale of our youth, have increased the tendencies to delinquent behavior. It is true that adult crimes have also increased at least as much. This fact has an important relation to youthful crime, but one comment must suffice here. When delinquency becomes habitual in a significant proportion of the young, it can be inferred that many of these young persons will graduate into adult criminality. On any accounting the situation is grievous and calls not simply for greater efforts and larger expenditures by our agencies, public and private, but even more, as we hope to show, for the development of a concerted strategy, based on the experience we have gained and on the findings of research.

Apart from those we have suggested, there is yet another reason why we must depend on broad estimates rather than on accurate measurements to assess changes in the volume of juvenile delinquency. Delinquency is a category that includes a large assortment of behavings, ranging from the merest pranks of high-spirited or adventurous youngsters to wanton crimes. It contains certain activities that are not legal offenses for adults: truancy, running away from home, insubordination to parents, endangering the health or morals of oneself or others (at least as this phrase is sometimes interpreted). Obviously so vaguely inclusive a category admits a great deal of discretion in the designation of youths as delinquent; according to the attitude of officials and the temper of the public the recorded amount of delinquency may fall or rise apart from any intrinsic change in the behavior of the young. Another important factor is the increase in traffic offenses, many of which consist in temporary "borrowing" of cars or motorcycles, illicit use of cars, and so forth. In the United States in 1961, traffic offenses constituted 27 per cent of all juvenile court cases.

Most youngsters at some time commit acts that can legally be designated delinquent. It is essential therefore to distinguish between the sporadic mischievousness of the young and the grow-ing habit of delinquent behavior. Judges have the responsibility of making this distinction before they designate a youth as de-linquent. They should also possess the capacity to diagnose the different types of delinquent behavior, though with crowded court calendars and the lack of training of some judges, this desideratum is too frequently lacking.

Skill in diagnosis is important at every stage in dealing with delinquency, which is by no means a simple or uniform malady. Various types are differently evoked, differently developed, and call for different approaches to treatment. It is no more pos-sible to prescribe the same treatment for the different problems of delinquent youth than it is for different diseases. Without careful diagnosis we cannot hope to provide effective treatment or give the requisite aid and guidance. In our study of delin-quency in New York City we were constantly impressed by the need for more careful screening before treatment. During that period (1958–1961) we found screening to be inadequate on all levels: by the police in their discretion to arrest, or to warn the offender and his parents, or to refer the case to an ap-propriate agency; by the courts in the process of adjudication and of disposition; by the probation division in the manner in which its members attempted to deal with their cases; by the institutions to which more serious offenders were committed; by the schools in their guidance and referral services, and also in their relegation of troublesome children to special schools or special classes; and by the welfare institutions in their programs of individual guidance and group therapy.[4]

If we are to control juvenile delinquency and redirect mis-guided youths we need a better understanding of their troubles and their responses to them. We need, in a word, an informed, concerted, and well-directed strategy. A main purpose of our study is to reveal this need and to offer suggestions for such a strategy.

2

High-Delinquency and
Low-Delinquency Areas

There is delinquency in all areas. It is always a question of degree. Charts and maps for New York City prepared under the writer's direction showed an irregular gradation in the number of delinquency cases between the highest and the lowest ranking areas. The gradation might well be more regular and less steep were it not for the advantage the better areas have in keeping their errant children from police notice, and from arrest when they are noticed.

Even in the finest residential areas we have occasional reports of wanton damage and riotous behavior by rampaging youth. A flagrant case followed a debutante party in Southampton, Long Island, on August 31 and September 1, 1963, when a mob of youths broke into a nearby beach house and proceeded to break things up, smashing windows and causing considerable destruction within the house. Four of the twenty or so youths involved were tried for vandalism, and acquitted. In 1965 a party of three hundred youths was invaded by the police as they were celebrating in an old house on the outskirts of the fashionable resort of East Hampton, and a number of them were held on charges varying from disorderly conduct to the possession or sale of narcotics. The Westchester Council of Social Agencies made a study of juvenile delinquency in some commuting areas and found the rates alarmingly high. A similar report comes from a commuter town in Connecticut. Obviously our official statistics present us with a somewhat one-sided picture of the situation. Since well-to-do parents are able and usually ready to make monetary reparation for vandalism and destruction by their children, such acts are likely to escape the courts.

Conditions in areas of relatively lower delinquency but in which there has also been some increase in delinquency, present a different problem from high-delinquency areas. In the latter we reasonably infer that the differential conditions, say, between high- and low-delinquency areas of a great city not only are correlated with the volume of delinquency but also are causally related to it. This conclusion will be pointed up in Part Two of this study. In areas of low delinquency the difference between present figures and the lower ones of earlier years is susceptible of several different explanations.

In the first place, it may be due to changes occurring specifically in the affected areas. Take, for example, the increase of delinquency in small towns. We could consider the impact of an increase of mobility, or of the stronger influence of big-city culture through television and other media of communication. The cultural urbanization of rural and small-town life might diminish the distinctive morality formerly bred in these latter areas, especially among the young. We would expect then that the towns in the hinterland of great cities would be more affected, and if a study of the relative increase in delinquency in the nearer and the more distant regions supported that conclusion the evidence would be important. We do not, however, know of any such study.

In the second place, the increase in delinquency in relatively low delinquency areas might be distributed very unequally and thus be attributable to special factors in the areas of greater increase. It is conceivable, for example, that commuter areas may have a higher tendency to juvenile delinquency, because of the father's absence from home during the whole day and sometimes the evening, or because of factors related to this mode of living. On the other hand, there is certainly evidence that some ethnic groups, especially where they are somewhat insulated by a thoroughly inculcated religious orthodoxy, tend to have lower delinquency rates while others have relatively high ones, so that the ethnic composition of an area would make a difference in the statistics.

In the third place, the relative increase shown in areas of lower delinquency may be due to the changing temper of the times everywhere. This interpretation would find a common ground for the over-all increase in juvenile delinquency in so many countries besides our own. For uncounted millions the decencies and usages of civil life were, during a long period of strain and anxiety, suspended and exchanged for the ugly necessities of killing and ravage. It was not to be expected that when that period ended people would resume their former modes of life and social attitudes. The experience of an age of unparalleled violence left its legacy of unrest, unbalance, and the confusion of morals. People were habituated to the lawlessness that goes with violence, and this has been reflected in the emphasis on violence presented through the media of mass communications—television, the movies, and the comics. The elders who have taken part in or lived through warfare are affected by their experience and this in turn is communicated to their children. Today we are confronted with the danger of another great war, which this time would obliterate total populations and destroy the civilization mankind has built through the ages. In such an atmosphere the sense of social cohesion is loosened, family ties are weakened, there is a general lowering of regard for spiritual and religious values. Crime increases, and juvenile delinquency climbs to new summits.

This type of explanation, with its various overtones, would not override the more special considerations that may account for the higher delinquency in areas subjected to particular pressures or disabilities, but it would, it is claimed, account for the over-all increase in every type of area. In Part Three we shall endeavor to sum up the case for this approach to the problem of causation.

Meanwhile we point out that not only in our high-delinquency areas but in all kinds of environments there occur the conjunctions of conditions that evoke or develop the more deep-seated maladjustments of youth. We have suggested that the volume of delinquency among upper-class youth is relatively greater than the statistics indicate—not only because the delinquency is more easily concealed and more frequently compounded, but also because the greater resources of the offenders can direct it into channels that do not directly bring it under the control of the law.

High delinquency occurs in areas of squalor and sheer poverty, with all the concomitants we have been indicating. If more delinquency is bred there, it is because all the young people in such areas are subjected to adverse conditions under which many of them are unable to accommodate themselves to lawful ways. In more favored areas many children find this accommodation relatively easy, but others, through a combination of unfortunate upbringing with a mental make-up that yields to the resulting vexations and disturbances, become no less maladjusted than those children of the slums. Two factors may be singled out as particularly important in conducing to delinquency in middle-class areas. One, which may be found in all areas, is the lack of home guidance or wise discipline—whether the failure be due to harsh treatment, the "spoiling" of the child because of inadequate restraint on wayward tendencies, neglect, or lack of affection. The importance of this factor has been brought out in many studies, and most notably by the Gluecks,[1] though their stress on it may not allow sufficiently for the environmental pressures that tend to disrupt family relationships. This subject will be examined more fully in a later section.

The other factor that looms up most significantly in middle-class areas is the pressure of the operative social code on resistant youth. By the operative code we mean the prescriptions inculcated by the values that rule everyday life. We distinguish it from the formal code of morality that prescribes the general rules of right behavior. The latter code is accepted, taught, and preached—and practiced within the limits of social decency. But it is the operative code that prescribes the strategy of living and tends to be followed even when it involves infractions of the formal moral code. Public pronouncements and exhortations to follow the formal code seem to be discounted compared with the inside pressures toward pursuit of the values of the operative code.[2] Foremost among these values, at least in the average middle-class circle, is the estimation of success, success in making good in business, in a career, in the more lucrative professions, in the process of "rising in the world."

There are always, however, deviant youths, who want to go their own way, perhaps to devote themselves to such unlucrative pursuits as art or music or drama, or who deride the cherished values of the business world, or who drift into becoming "playboys." Sometimes in these situations the tensions arising in the home are heightened by neurotic or temperamental tendencies in the youth, who may then resort to delinquent habits.

The young people of middle-class or upper-class neighborhoods are no more immune than those of the slums from the behavior problems or psychic disturbances that may result in confirmed delinquency, especially when they do not receive the wise guidance and skilled treatment that might redirect their aggressiveness or waywardness into more constructive activities. Well-to-do parents, no less than poor parents, may fail to understand their children's problems. In many instances, perhaps particularly with the commuting class, they see less of their children than do slum parents. Some crucial situation, such as an unfortunate sexual experience or a school failure or a foolish debt incurred by the youth, may trigger the fatal collision between parent and child that ends in the latter's dedication to rebelliousness and the total rejection of authority. Occasionally the press reports a serious crime committed by a youth—or youths—who seemed to have every advantage of fortune, revealing a glimpse of some deep disorder beneath the surface. The most famous of such cases was that of Leopold and Loeb, who out of prurient curiosity and unmitigated sadism murdered a child. With every gift of position and intelligence these two had escaped the discipline and lacked the guidance that might have averted the tragedy.

There is no class distinction in the need for watchful guidance in a spirit of affection. The crucial situation that marks the parting of the ways between an honorable or a delinquent career occurs in every environment. We were impressed a number of years ago by a report on a confirmed delinquent who had been a handsome and happy youngster, well-behaved and successful at school. In an accident at play the point of a knife pierced an eye, and the resulting disfigurement preyed on his feelings so that he became morose and withdrawn, lost interest in his work and play, and ended as an adjudged delinquent. One could but surmise what a difference it might have made if some sympathetic and understanding counselor had been with him through the time of crisis.

High Delinquency Areas—
The Complex of Residence and Residents

A considerable amount of research has been devoted to the conditions associated with delinquency, both the conditions under which individual cases occur and those of areas in which the volume of delinquency is high or above average. Since individual cases are excessively variant and often quite complex, we shall consider at this stage the latter line of inquiry, especially as it throws considerable light on the former.

There is everywhere a marked disparity between the amount of juvenile delinquency recorded in the various areas of cities, and the highest volume is nearly always found in the poorest sectors. This fact raises two preliminary questions. In the first place, every area combines two major constituents: the physical environment itself, with its housing conditions, its amenities or lack thereof, its higher or lower rental values, and so forth; and also the demographic aspect—the characteristics of the groups who inhabit it, their wealth or poverty, their social status, their ethnic derivation, and so on. Should we then attribute the higher or lower delinquency rates to one or to the other of these factors, or again to the combination of the two? Has either factor priority over the other as an explanation of the delinquency level?

Different answers have been given. We shall pay special attention to these questions in Part Two, when we face the problem of causation.

In the second place, we must ask whether the statistical disparity itself is a genuine index of the relative volume of delinquency in the higher delinquency areas, or is it at least in part a reflection of the greater risk of detection and police arrest and partially also of the treatment and process of adjudication after arrest? There is no doubt that the chances of detection are greater in poor areas where the playground is usually the street and the meeting place the street corner or the candy store. Chances of arrest are greater where parents are not influential, where the youth may be subject to police discrimination (so many in the poorer areas today are Puerto Ricans or Negroes), where he has no one to plead his case in court, or, since most juvenile cases are conducted without legal defense, has parents who are unable to present an effective argument on his behalf. We must therefore discount any pretension that the statistical disparity is a true differential of the actual amounts of delinquency prevalent in slum areas and in well-to-do areas respectively. It must be remembered again that quite a considerable volume of delinquency everywhere escapes police notice, and the chance of escaping is better in the more secluded retreats of well-to-do youngsters.

Nevertheless, the actual preponderance of juvenile delinquency in low-income neighborhoods is well confirmed by various studies. We take as example a recent study by Reiss and Rhodes.[3] They took a base population of 9,238 white boys aged twelve and over, registered during the 1957 school year in a public, a private, and a parochial school of Davidson County, Tennessee. A delinquent was identified as a boy adjudged delinquent before the Davidson County Juvenile Court. The study showed that the delinquency rate increased as one moved down the line from high to low IQ and from "white collar" to "blue collar" occupations. The disparity is greater for serious than for petty offenses, and considerably greater also for truancy, so often associated with delinquent tendencies. It is a reasonable assumption that under any conditions the more serious offenses are less likely to be overlooked or condoned than the petty ones. The only charge for which the "white collar" rate was higher than the "blue collar" was traffic offenses, for pretty obvious reasons. Another significant fact brought out by the Reiss-Rhodes study is that "the delinquency life-chances of *all* status groups tend to be greatest in the lower-status area and in the high-delinquency areas."

Incidentally, as these authors point out, the evidence just cited is adverse to the theory that juvenile delinquency of the more pronounced sort is a factor or an aspect of "lower-class morality" or "lower-class culture," whether as spontaneously bred within it, or as due to the ineffective effort of lower-class youth to live up to "middle-class norms"—conclusions with which we shall be concerned in a latter part of this study.

Everywhere, seemingly, there is more recorded delinquency in the lower-class areas, but this again is too broad and heterogeneous a bracketing to serve our inquiry. Further analysis shows that high incidence is concentrated in particular localities or pockets of the large city, while some lower-class areas show about average delinquency, and a few distinctly less than average. In certain higher-status areas, including some newer suburbs of great cities, delinquency is well above average for that type of area. What therefore is significant is not the broad attribution of greater delinquency to lower-class areas as such but the discovery of the delinquency-breeding conditions characterizing areas where delinquency is most rife.

The pockets of high delinquency within a larger urban area offer us an important approach to the study and understanding of youthful delinquency as a whole. The disparity between the rates for these areas and for others is usually sustained over long periods, in spite of the mobility of their populations. It would therefore seem reasonable to assume that the differential response of youth to the conditions existing within these areas is due, at least in part, to the impact of these conditions on their attitudes, habits, and aspirations. However, the populations of the high-delinquency areas are characteristically groups of in-migrants coming from backgrounds very different from that of the city, and the evidence we possess indicates that in their previous environments the young people did not exhibit any comparable tendency to delinquency. A study of the activities of delinquency-prone youth in high-delinquency areas may thus throw some light on the state of mind that, even though evoked under very different conditions, leads young persons elsewhere to be defiant of authority and disposed to resort to illegal ways.

When we seek to understand the disparity between high-delinquency and low-delinquency areas we must realize that the social pathology indicated by high delinquency is one aspect of a vital situation characterized not only by squalid and congested living conditions but also by other sociopathological features. The public has been too much disposed to regard juvenile delinquency as a gratuitous expression of youthful wrongdoing, something to be corrected simply by more discipline, more severe penalties, more vigorous action by the police and the courts. When, however, we appreciate the manner in which the high-delinquency areas are correlated to various other social evils that obviously call for a different approach, we should see how deeply such delinquency is rooted in a matrix of serious social maladjustment affecting youths and adults alike. Even less helpful is the occasional demand that the parents be penalized for the offenses of their offspring. Clearly something more fundamental than "mere correction" is necessary, even if we still attach some importance to that mode of treatment.

Sociopathological Concomitants

Evidence from many sources indicates an association between high delinquency and other social maladies, but we shall here concentrate on the results of an intensive study in the City of New York made by its Juvenile Delinquency Evaluation Project under the direction of the writer.[4] We compared the delinquency rates of the thirty health center areas of the City with a series of indices of health disabilities and related conditions, and with another series for economic disabilities. We had thus nine variables in all, as follows: admissions to New York State mental hospitals, terminations of psychiatric clinic cases, active tuberculosis cases, infant mortality, out-of-wedlock live births, public assistance cases (all relief cases coming under the New York City Welfare Department), aid to dependent children (Federal-State programs to aid widowed or divorced mothers), home-relief cases (a State-City relief program for cases that do not qualify under the standard categories of the Federal program), together with a composite Health Department Index combining four categories; cases of children for whom no dental care was reported, relative prevalence of tuberculosis, percentage of total births to ward patients who had no private physician, and gonorrhea cases.

The outstanding fact was that delinquency rates showed throughout a remarkable concomitant variation with our nine other indices. There were minor exceptions and discrepancies. The indices for admissions to mental-health hospitals and for termination of psychiatric clinic cases showed some spotty nonconformities with the other seven indices; a few areas showed higher ratings for delinquency than for most of the other variables. But the trend to co-variation between delinquency and all other indices was significant, and the three areas that headed the delinquency index were at or near the top of all the other indices.

Evidently we have here a vicious circle of troubles. Morbidity in all its forms is somehow associated with high delinquency, though we cannot yet assume any direct causal relationships, and delinquency in turn is closely associated with other socio-psychological phenomena. We have then the alternative hypotheses that the initiation of the vicious circle lies in one or in the combination of, say, two, of the associated factors, or else that behind them all there is some fundamental condition that is the prime mover of the whole series. Once set going, the vicious circle may sustain itself by mutual interactions, with the continued support of the fundamental condition itself. We may look for the fundamental condition in the slum environment occupied by the people suffering from these evils. Certainly high-delinquency areas are almost invariably slum areas, areas of excessive populational congestion, characterized by a substantial percentage of dilapidated dwelling units, uncared-for and deteriorating, in official terms "substandard and insanitary," and lacking in park and playground facilities, where nothing but abject poverty meets the eye.

This hypothesis receives considerable support when we examine, as we shall proceed to do, the manner in which this type of slum environment creates, under the comparative stresses of American society, extremely difficult problems for the young people reared within it. Such an environment is a serious handicap, thrusting back and then dulling the aspirations initially stimulated by the mores of more prosperous neighborhoods around them.

The Physical Environment and the Group Culture

Important as the impact of the physical environment is, it offers no adequate explanation of the social phenomenon appearing within it. A Chicago school of sociologists used to point out that successive groups of immigrants, of different background and ethnic origin, exhibited a similar tendency to relatively high delinquency when they occupied in turn the same physically deteriorating areas of the city—the "zones of transition" where industrial invasion disrupted residential neighborhoods. It must be remembered, however, that these successive groups have usually been disprivileged and rather destitute entrants, unused to the life and ways of the large city, subject to exploitation, disorganized, and exposed to social and economic discrimination. Thus we cannot impute the resultant social phenomena to the physical environment alone, and closer examination always reveals some differences of response by incoming groups of different cultural backgrounds. Each group brings with it its own predispositions, habituations, folkways, and problems. These characteristics undergo modifications under the strains of the new environment, the influence of which is usually much stronger on the young. Southern Negroes settling in a northern city enter with long-established habituations to American traditions. Their language and their general culture are those of their new home, except for minor variations developed during their segregated existence in the South. They have had lifelong relations with white Americans, even if these have often been unfavorable ones. Puerto Ricans, on the other hand, enter the same type of environment with a very different cultural experience, are for the most part unfamiliar with English, and quite unversed in the ways of our urban society. In New York City they dwell in the same kind of physical environment as the southern Negroes, often side by side in the same neighborhood, but we see some indications that their response is in some respects rather different from that of the latter group. They show less tendency to aggressive group protests, seem rather more likely to take refuge in escapist accommodations, and are more prone to narcotic addiction.

In sharp contrast to both these groups are the rigidly orthodox Hasidic Jews, who settled in Williamsburg, an area of Brooklyn where they live with Puerto Ricans and others. The Hasidim reject all contacts with the Puerto Ricans and indeed with all other groups, including an older Jewish group that has gradually been moving out of the neighborhood. They carry with them powerful indoctrinations and bring up their children under the most rigorous and exclusive training in the faith. They have a profound conviction of their own moral superiority and of the unique rightness of their doctrine, with its elaborate rituals and ceremonial observances, with its distinctive and peculiar requirements of dress and demeanor. They have succeeded in keeping the majority of their youth almost untouched by the influences around them, and among other features of this group is a low rate of juvenile delinquency. Similarly, for a long period the Chinese community in a small crowded area in Manhattan, living in its own way and cherishing its own usages in the midst of a community that was wholly indifferent and alien to it, exhibited a remarkable absence of juvenile delinquency. There are indications, however, that under the slow permeation of outside influences some tendency to delinquency has now developed.

Clearly, then, the ethos, standards, and social cohesion of the groups migrating into our congested city areas affect their responses to the new conditions and are a determinant of the degree of resistance they exhibit to the disadvantages and pressures of the physical environment. The examples of effective resistance we possess strongly suggest that two great social bulwarks against the breakdown of youthful morale within an adverse environment are, first, the group's conviction of its own values, of the superiority of its standards, making it in large measure proof against the frustrations and confusions of life in an alien and unpropitious situation, and second, an authoritative family system which inculcates these values in the young from their earliest years. One great danger to which most of our inmigrant groups are exposed is the rankling insecurity that comes from a sense of inferiority, or of imputed inferiority.

An interesting sidelight on the effect that the strength of a group's values and standards has on the behavior of its members in an adverse environment is available in records of the hideous Nazi concentration camps. A young sociologist, Paul Neurath, son of a distinguished Viennese scholar, spent many months interned in one of these camps. He surreptitiously made careful notes on the different ways the various classes of victims behaved under the brutal and degrading treatment they received. In this preoccupation, he explained, he himself found some respite from the continuous horror of the situation. It was easy to spot to which of the rejected classes any individual belonged, since each of the seven or eight categories of prisoners wore a differently colored badge. The categories included political prisoners of the Gestapo; professional criminals; vagrants and others who had gotten into trouble with the Nazi social agencies; unacceptable emigrants who had been brought back to Germany or for some reason had returned of themselves (these were mostly Jews); "race polluters" (also mainly Jewish); homosexuals; and Jehovah's Witnesses. Dr. Neurath's evidence showed that the groups with the strongest sense of group identification and group standards were the ones that best resisted the disintegrating effects of their treatment, that were least liable

to break down under it.[5] Highest in the list stood the wearers
of the blue triangle, Jehovah's Witnesses, a group animated by
the absolute conviction that God was at their side. They refused
to break down and only among them were there no suicides.
They were followed in ranking by the socialist-communist
groups. Lowest on the list were the wearers of the black triangle,
the vagrants and those who had got into trouble on their jobs
or had not kept their employment—a group officially designated
the "asocial."

The conditions experienced by most of the groups that have
migrated to our great cities, who come to better their lot and
start on the lowest economic level, have been such as to undermine the assurances and aspirations of the members of their
groups, especially the young members. Lacking cohesion, disorganized, their former ways of life disrupted because of their
inability to adapt to the new conditions, their value systems de-
ranged by conflict with the values of the surrounding community, unappreciated and discriminated against, they struggle
against considerable odds for some kind of integrity, and the
amount of juvenile delinquency is a register of the degree in
which they are unsuccessful. The history of New York City,
with its successive waves of in-migrants, shows that the newest
arrivals have always lacked adequate protection against the
stresses and handicaps of the slum environments which the
additional congestion caused by arrival inevitably worsened. It
was so with Jewish groups, Irish groups, Eastern European
groups, and Southern Italians. Now it is the turn of the southern
Negroes and the Puerto Ricans. Now it is these who suffer from
disorientation, and this disorientation is intensified by the prejudice and discrimination they encounter from the older established residents. Groups that are economically insecure are thus
rendered socially insecure as well, and the morale of the young
is too severely tried.

The Pressures of the Environment on Social Relationships

With these considerations in mind, we can now briefly consider some adverse influences on youthful morale specifically arising from slum environments. The observations that follow are primarily the result of the writer's own experience with children and families exposed to these conditions, though they are borne out by many other studies.

In the first place, the sheer congestion of slum life is adverse to the aspirations of youth. Opportunities of every kind are restricted or lacking. The crowded family gives the youth no place of retreat, no quiet in which he can prepare his homework for school, no privacy. There are no books, no pictures that matter. There is seldom anyone with whom he can discuss his problems. For release he must go out to the street; in cold weather he crowds into the candy store. Often he has no outlet for his energies except in noise-making, rowdiness, and mischievous pranks.

It is symptomatic of his situation that he often finds the street more pleasant than the home. There are no influences around to teach him good manners or good speech. So, when he goes into the school, he already carries a handicap with him. His teachers speak a different language. He is unfamiliar with their type of teaching. He misses much of what they would teach and vainly tries to conceal the fact. His background, his upbringing, are all against his success. The teacher is likely to conclude that he has little learning capacity and tends to treat him accordingly. He is labeled as low IQ. He is often mechanically passed along from grade to grade, learning very little in the process.

The children of slums suffer multiple disadvantages in their schooling. Except for some dedicated ones, the better teachers naturally prefer to be placed elsewhere. The low standards, and perhaps even more the fact that the children seem unresponsive and sometimes are rowdy or troublesome, make most teachers unwilling to stay in slums if they can possibly find other positions. The schools are populated mainly by the children of the in-migrant groups. If the pupils are Puerto Ricans, they have little facility with the English language. In consequence they miss much that they are taught and are usually retarded in reading, the most serious of all retardations. The southern Negroes, the other large migrant group, are an equally bad case. Their education before their arrival in northern schools has usually been deplorable. Where, as in various neighborhoods, they constitute the majority of the school population, there is a momentum of helplessness and inertia in the face of schooling requirements. Sometimes they come to school having had too little sleep during late wasted nights at home or on the street, or they arrive burdened with the troubles from which their parents are suffering. They have already learned that they are the objects of discrimination, and nothing is more calculated to depress their ambitions as well as their prospects.

Failure in school, from whatever causes, has not only a numbing effect on youthful aspirations and on the chances of a career, it is also associated with the formation of habits and attitudes adverse to morale. Retardation leads to truancy and truants become school drop-outs. It breeds frustration and the tendency to rebel against authority. In New York City schools, reports show only 62.4 per cent of those who entered the ninth grade in 1951 were graduated in due course from academic high school; only 37.6 of vocational high school students were graduated.[6] The drop-out rate for boys was even higher, only 59 per cent graduating from academic high school and 34 per cent from vocational school. Most of the more disturbed pupils go to vocational high schools if they continue school at all, and they begin dropping out in a steady stream from the outset.[7]

The significance of these figures is registered in the delinquency statistics. Many of the children who appear before the juvenile courts are charged with chronic truancy in addition to other offenses, and truancy itself is often the first stage in the process that leads to persistent delinquency. The high correlation between school retardation and delinquency has been shown in a number of studies.[8] It is significant also that reading retardation has been found to be correlated with some of the other environmental and sociopathological conditions we have shown to be characteristic of the high-delinquency areas.[9]

The school is next to the family as a determinant of the outlook of the young and their consequent life-chances. And when trouble at school is combined with troubles within the slum family, these conditions interact, each tending to magnify the effect of the other and increasing the likelihood of delinquency. The environmental and sociopathological troubles disturb the life of the family and make it less congenial to the young. The relations between parents and children are in grave danger of being impaired. Rifts develop more easily, and often enough the parents (or one of them) take the wrong ways of dealing with the situation. It is not only in the "broken family" that home life is imperiled, but also and not less in the family that has suffered some demoralization under the impact of a complex of troubles. Even in happier circumstances the concord of parents and offspring is subject to tests that it may not be able to withstand. In the much more difficult and trying conditions of life in high-delinquency areas, it would certainly not be surprising if failure occurred more frequently.

To some students of the subject, juvenile delinquency is the consequence of bad family upbringing, and certainly no one can dispute the great role played by the early formative influences of the family and the kind and degree of training provided within it. The Gluecks have made the relations between parents and children and the "cohesion" of the family the basis of their predictive scale. The limitation and defects of this scale have been sufficiently pointed out; in any event what is called the cohesion of the family may be disturbed or disrupted both by forces operating from without the family and by crises within it for which the family itself cannot be held responsible. Young persons generally have a resilience that can resist many adverse influences, and it is preferable to regard the development of delinquent tendencies as caused by a complex of disturbing conditions. The transition from mere occasional or sporadic acts of delinquency to a confirmed bent toward delinquent behavior is frequently triggered by some crucial event—a gross disillusionment, a rebuff, a stigma, or whatever it may be. But this is a subject we must follow up in Part Two.

Besides the home and the school there is the street. The

clutter and frequent uncongeniality of the home lead young people to spend all the more time on the street, where what they see and hear is often harsh and ugly. They fall in with others of their kind. They have no sandlots or open spaces or available playgrounds where they might employ their energies in zestful games. They are on the lookout for something to do, and the most aggressive or "acting-out" member is likely to make himself the leader and induce the others to join him in exploits that often enough take on a law-breaking character. The group of boys who under other conditions would form a team becomes a street-corner gang. The education provided by the slum street is no training in manners or in morals.

The only place many of these boys feel at home is the street, where they can act and feel like themselves among their own kind. The school is unpleasant and discouraging—though there are now some happy exceptions. The home is troubled, often depressing, sometimes quarrelsome. What alternative have they? But the street is a place of dangers. It is a hang-out of undesirable characters. A drunkard staggers along, and may arouse the cruelty of untamed youth who take advantage of his incapacity. A bully or a homosexual or a dope peddler may accost them. One of the boys may have a brother in a neighboring gang and give the others ideas about following this lead into illicit adventures. If the boys are Negroes, they may get into trouble with Puerto Ricans, or vice versa. There may be other "alien" groups—Irish, Italian, Polish, or Jewish—who jeer at them or harass them. The street breeds more hate than love of one's neighbors.

Though the street is the inevitable resort of boys in slum areas, it is far from being either a pleasant or a desirable alternative for the facilities they lack. Much of the time it is uncomfortable because of bad weather, forcing the boys to huddle in alleys or hallways or to crowd into candy stores or other refuges. When they do gather in a knot on the street, the police are likely to tell them to move or scatter. They may be charged with "unlawful assembly." They come to regard the police as their natural enemies. One way or another they are liable to get into trouble and in consequence they come both to fear authority and to lose respect for it, an attitude that is conducive to evasive law-breaking.

Brought up in such surroundings, the boys are ill prepared to meet the demands of the future. There are two ways in particular in which their present condition and the attitudes it breeds tend to jeopardize their future welfare. In the first place, their growing interest in sex creates a problem. What they learn about it on the streets, from older boys and in casual conversations among themselves, is usually coarse, indecent, and ugly. Even little boys indulge in bawdy language; it is a sign of youthful manlinesss. The more decent girls of the neighborhood do not consort with the boys on the street. The occasional girl who does is likely to have a tendency toward promiscuity and to be ready to proceed with one or more of them to a dark alley or roof. There is no real companionship and little enough pleasure in these casual relationships, illicitly snatched in drab and degrading situations. They constitute an unhappy preparation for genuine love-making and the more enduring satisfactions that might follow.

The second danger to their future well-being is related to the first. Backward or retarded in their schooling, they are ready to abandon it as soon as possible, often before they reach the age prescribed by law. In this way and in others they are unprepared for steady employment. In our time it is hard enough even for the better equipped slum boys to find jobs. Their manners and modes of speech, often their race or ethnic origin, are against them. So, at an age when it is peculiarly dangerous to live precariously in enforced idleness, these youths, dulled in their aspirations and frustrated in their hopes, drift toward a blank future.

It should be sufficiently clear from these abbreviated comments that in itself the physical environment in which a high rate of delinquency prevails has a seriously adverse affect on the life chances of the young people growing up in it. While many somehow are able to overcome its worst dangers and become decent members of the community, these areas remain breeding grounds for delinquency and no salvage measures can do more than partially mitigate their perils.

In short, only the thorough rehabilitation of these areas, along with the creation of opportunities for the proper equipment of their youth as responsible adults, can effectively meet the present challenge of the slums.

3

The Psychic Conditions

"How does it happen that some young people living in the same family environment as the delinquent . . . are able to refrain from anti-social contact?" This was the question asked by William Healy and Augusta F. Bronner in their distinctive and path-finding volume *New Light on Delinquency and Its Treatment*.[1] They focused attention on the psychology of delinquency, whereas earlier study of high-delinquency areas was in a narrower sense sociological—concerned, that is, with relating the incidence of delinquency to the conditions of the inclusive social environment, the neighborhood or urban area. It was obvious enough that within this social milieu there must be more intimate conditions to account for the fact that so many youthful residents even of the worst areas, did not become delinquent. Healy and Bronner found the differential factor in the family situation. It was mainly for them a matter of the sociopsychological adjustments of youth to familial relations within the broader context of the higher-delinquency environment.

There is certainly a convincing volume of evidence to confirm the Healy and Bronner position that the lack of sustaining close relationships of affection and trust between parent and child in the latter's early years is a delinquency-provoking factor of first importance. These authors maintained that where the parent-child tie was emotionally strong, a basis of satisfaction was constructed on which a pattern of socially acceptable habits and attitudes would in all probability be built, notwithstanding the adverse pressures of the inclusive environment. The rapport established between parent and child, even if the parent were not intrinsically worthy, made possible an adjustment that could override adverse influences from without. Along these lines, which many later writers have followed with variations, our authorities filled a lacuna and thus revised previous imputations of delinquency primarily to the physical environment and its impact on youth. Observe, however, that the new approach still placed the emphasis on environment—on the nearer and differential environment of the family situation.

This solution, however significant, was by no means the last word. It was criticized on two grounds. In the first place, it was claimed that the evidences submitted could not themselves bear the total weight of so absolute a conclusion. Queries were raised about the representativeness of the selected sample, composed of 105 delinquents and 105 nondelinquent siblings—all referral cases from the courts to diagnostic or guidance units attached to these courts. The preliminary court selection of the cases might render them unrepresentative of the court cases as a whole. Beyond this, however, the study could not answer a more far-reaching question. When our authors concluded that over 90 per cent of the delinquent cases exhibited grave discontent or extreme disturbance caused by their family experiences or life circumstances, the question still open was how far psychic deficiencies, congenital or a result of early neglect, maltnutrition, or physical damage of some kind, may have weakened resistance to unfavorable experiences. We note that 13 per cent of the sibling controls were also reported to have exhibited mental stress and disturbances. Did these then have a greater capacity to withstand the delinquency-provoking experiences to which the others succumbed? May there not be a gradient of capacity for social adjustment under stress that involves not only the experiential history of the individual but also his psychological make-up and the circumstances attending its early development?

It is important to observe that these qualifications in no way invalidate the findings of Healy and Bronner and of the many other researchers who have similarly reported on the relation of early home experiences to the presence or absence of delinquency. However, other causative factors must be reckoned with if we are to approach a fuller understanding of why some young persons become delinquent and others do not. Causation is a many-sided affair; other approaches than the psychological and the sociological have something to contribute to the solution of the complex problems of prevention and treatment. For practical purposes it is important to know that in a very large number of cases the lack of a strong emotional tie between parents and children evokes delinquent tendencies in the child. This understanding opens the way for more intelligent treatment and gives leads for more hopeful efforts in prevention. But certainly in a considerable number of cases remedial help can be sought from the pediatrist and the specialist in neurotic and psychosomatic ailments. And there are of course particular categories, such as the psychotic and the mentally deficient, for which only specialist treatment can be of much service.

Other professional groups have also found the roots of delinquency in the near environment—in the family and the early upbringing of the child. This approach is pre-eminently that of the psychoanalysts. They agree generally with most psychologists, social psychologists, and psychiatrists in emphasizing disturbances that occur in the early socialization of the child. The psychoanalysts are distinctive, however, in the role they assign to unconscious motivation, to the suppressed "instincts" of childhood that find expression in neurotic anxieties and wayward behavior. The human infant is at first an animal directed to the satisfaction of its animal instincts. It is asocial and becomes socialized as experience and indoctrination exercise control over the purely "instinctive" nature. If this process is successfully carried out, the "ideal ego" or the "superego," at first very weak, develops and takes over. But failures occur in the process and the superego may remain weak. The suppressed desires take their revenge in various ways, delinquency being one of them.

An early leader in the psychoanalytic interpretation of delinquency was the Viennese psychoanalyst, August Aichhorn, who set up his own home for delinquents. He found in the frustrated yearning for love and affection the basis of delinquent behavior, and he believed that a system of persistent, friendly, permissive care was best calculated to bring about readjustment. For Aichhorn a large part of the problem is the enabling of the delinquent to achieve "identification" with the therapist. He claimed that the results achieved by his institution were excellent.

Aichhorn's work had considerable influence, and it has been followed up by promising experiments in treatment along the lines he pioneered. A notable example was Fritz Redl's Pioneer House, which took a group of extremely difficult boys and found that they responded well to treatment, showing an increased capacity to deal with their problems. Pioneer House, however, was closed before, in Redl's judgment, the experiment was completed.[2]

In other experiments less favorable results were reported. An example of the latter kind was the experiment in "milieu" therapy along Aichhorn's lines undertaken with a group of girls at Hawthorne–Cedar Knolls residential center. (A thorough investigation of the conditions under which one experiment succeeds and another fails might prove revealing.)

The psychoanalytic viewpoint has influenced many investigators who would not class themselves as adhering to the psychoanalytic school. The emphasis on the importance of the conditioning the child receives in its earliest years, not least in infancy, is widely accepted, and psychonalytic concepts such as "superego" and "transference" are used somewhat freely. There is, however, a primary distinction between the viewpoint of psychoanalysis and that generally held in other disciplines. The psychoanalyst regards delinquency as the expression of natural instincts which are normally brought under control in the socialization process. Sociologists and psychologists, on the other hand, commonly regard delinquency as the reaction of the child to conditions that deny him primary psychic or emotional satisfactions, thus creating or at least evoking antisocial attitudes. From this viewpoint, delinquents are made so, whereas to the psychoanalyst they are born so. If the latter viewpoint is taken we might find some kind of contradiction in the permissive modes of treatment many psychoanalysts have approved.

In the main, it is to the psychological researchers we must turn for our knowledge of the differential mental characteristics that underlie delinquent behavior. A good deal of knowledge on the types of malfunction, the area of disturbance, that result in juvenile delinquency, has been advanced in the studies of Fritz Redl. Psychologists are particularly concerned with the processes of personality growth and with the influences on personality development that evoke deviant forms of behavior. Some psychologists have given special attention, as Healy and Bronner did, to the role of deprivation and frustration in childhood and to the variant reactions to those conditions that depend on differences of mental or constitutional type. Psychological studies of personality changes at the outset of puberty and through adolescence are serviceable for the understanding of delinquency that manifests itself in the early teens. Another type of psychological inquiry has been the classification of personality types, but while it is convenient to make broad distinctions, the total personality is so complex and has so many aspects, there are so many combinations of attributes of varying degrees of strength as well as so many changes in the course of a life history, that every classification has its problems and none has become authoritative. This statement is also applicable to the various classifications of the delinquent personality.

For practical purposes, we need some simple *ad hoc* classifications, especially to screen cases prior to disposition and treatment. In looking through the intake records of certain institutions, the writer was struck by the frequency with which the term "disturbed" appeared, usually qualified by adjectives such as "very," "emotionally," "severely." So vague and inclusive a term has no diagnostic value. It might even be applied to delinquents who are reasonably well adjusted within the delinquent associations, though causing considerable disturbance otherwise. It is certainly applied both to delinquents who are chafing under the restraints imposed on them and to those who are suffering from a deeper-seated mental trouble. A clarification of the common vocabulary of those who work with delinquents is certainly needed.

One or two terms have become fairly well defined, among them "psychopathic." One definition, offered by William and Joan McCord, is: "The psychopath is an a-social, aggressive, highly impulsive person who feels little or no guilt and is unable to form lasting bonds of affection with other human beings."[3] The typical delinquent psychopath is full of unreasoning hostility; Fritz Redl described his psychopathic boys (our appellation, not his) as "the children who hate." The identification of this type (with its several varieties) is well confirmed in studies by Robert Lindner, Kate Friedlander, R. D. Rabinowitch, Lauretta Bender, and others. Many of these studies insist on the role of early rejection, emotional starvation, or brutal treatment in evoking the psychopathic features. "In study after study," say the McCords, "emotional deprivation appeared to have precipitated a psychopathic personality structure." This conclusion does not preclude the existence of congenital or constitutional mental disorders, glandular irregularities, or even initial psychic tendencies that may develop as a result of emotional shock; but the cases that have been recorded of successful treatment indicate that a socializing therapy can be applied with rather good prospects of success. The interdependence of bodily and mental functioning within the organism is so intimate that we can learn only from tested experience how far one or another therapeutic approach is of avail.

From the psychopathic type we must distinguish the psychotic. When we speak of the psychotic we imply a more deep-seated mental disorder, probably rooted in congenital mental defect, though, as in the schizophrenic, it may not reveal itself in the earlier life history. The psychotic has persistent delusions, cannot grapple with reality, and lives in the clouded world of a distorted imagination. He is often beset with anxiety and in some form of trouble, with a sense of shame or guilt, in which respect he is markedly different from the typical psychopath. Nor is he likely to be responsive to the therapeutic processes that have already been applied with some success to the psychopath.

Before leaving the subject of classification, let us cite a division proposed by Albert J. Reiss, Jr., which has attracted considerable interest since its publication in the *American Sociological Review* (December 1952). The article is entitled "Social Correlates of Psychological Types of Delinquency," and we might at the outset raise a question about that title. We doubt whether we should speak at all of "psychological types." If the phrase implies a classification of types of delinquent behavior on a psychological basis, almost all classifications are in terms of personality traits and thus could be called psychological, while in this particular classification the terms belong to the special approach of the psychoanalyst. But this initial cavil has nothing to do with the merits of the classification. It is a significant departure from other modes of classification, for Reiss suggests interesting correlations between delinquency types and types of environment.

The classification is threefold. The first category is that of the "relatively integrated" delinquent. He is pretty much in command of himself and "in all probability will become a mature, independent adult." He is a normally capable person, who can behave perfectly well when it suits him, and his lack of morals does not imply serious personal demoralization. The second category comprises delinquents with "relatively weak ego controls." It contains highly insecure persons with low self-esteem, and also highly aggressive and hostile youngsters. Both are unstable, having weak associations with their fellows, erratic, suffering from a sense of strain, with no clear standards of behavior. The third category contains "defective superego" delinquents. These have failed to make the code of the larger society their own, to "internalize" it, and thus have no qualms of conscience over their transgressions. They pay little regard to instruction and have poor records in every respect, usually drifting into whatever chance unskilled employment is available.

The first type, we are told, is usually found in the less desirable residential areas, in families that show little place mobility and are stable, respectable, conventional. The youth himself is not troublesome at school, usually attains high school level, and then finds regular employment. His offenses are mainly burglary and larceny, the stealing of automobiles being characteristic. He gets into trouble with the police and the court at a later age than do the other two types.

The "weak ego" type is usually found in well-established residential areas, but comes from a family that frequently moves from place to place. The parents, usually native-born, are not separated but their relationship is marked by serious conflicts; they tend to disregard conventional standards. The child is likely to be a habitual truant, but of average scholarship. He differs from the other two types in his low concern for peer-group association. He gets into trouble at a very early age. His characteristic offenses are wanton destruction and flouting authority.

The "defective superego" type is characteristically found in the poorer, dilapidated, urban areas. The family is not mobile. It is often broken, with parental conflict where both parents are present, and usually includes many children who lack any proper control and easily get into trouble. Truancy is very common, and police and court troubles begin at an early age.

We have spelled out this distinctive set of correlations between delinquency types and environmental factors because it suggests various lines of study that might considerably refine our understanding of the relation between delinquency and both the nearer and the more inclusive environments of the delinquent. The correlations themselves are based on an analysis of the court records of 1,110 white male probationers of the Juvenile Court of Cook County, Illinois, for 1943 and 1944. The data on which the study drew were compiled by psychiatric social workers and psychiatrists of the Institute for Juvenile Research, and the second and third categories were so classified by IJR psychiatrists.

This kind of seminal study leaves us with a variety of question marks. To the outsider the line between the "weak ego" type and the "defective superego" type is not clear, and he may not be sure that the actual decision to put delinquents into one or the other category is sufficiently authoritative. There might, for example, be a tendency to classify a candidate as "defective superego" because he comes from a broken home and is a gang member and lives in a deteriorated area and did not complete his grade school education. But all these symptoms may be related to special conditions, and they are not themselves definitive of a "defective superego." We assume that the classification was made with scholarly care; our point is that, when the correlates which appear to be associated with a type are much more specific and well demarcated than the type itself, the problem of classification has unusual risks. Our main conclusion is that Dr. Reiss has in a most suggestive way exposed an hypothesis concerning the different aspects and forms of delinquency responsible to different social and physical environments.

Standing apart from those who relate the various manifestations of delinquency to differences in mentality or personality, is a small group which finds in the "body type"—the physical constitution—a basis for classifying mentalities that in turn gives clues to delinquent tendencies. A pioneer in this field was William H. Sheldon, but his work was eclectic and somewhat confused, and was ruled out of court in a devastating critique by the leading criminologist, Edwin H. Sutherland. The subject, however, was taken up by the indefatigable Gluecks in their volume entitled *Physique and Delinquency* (New York, 1956). They limited their claim to the proposition that some of the mental traits associated with delinquency are also associated with a particular type of physique. The "mesomorph" type, the athletic, tough, strong-bodied frame, appears to have a greater tendency to delinquency than the other two types. Such tentative conclusions are not without interest, but they do not offer much that is serviceable either for the understanding or for the control of delinquency. From time to time someone discovers a correlation between some physiological differentia and the proneness to delinquency. A physician attached to an important medical institution once showed the writer a series of photographs that revealed a divergence between the formation of the knee joints of a group of delinquents from that characteristic of the age group in general. The evidence was there, for what it was worth, but it was not, so far as the writer knows, supported by wider investigation.

To sum up, we have sought in this first part to survey the nature of the problem posed for all who endeavor to understand why delinquency is more incident to some groups than to others, to some localities than to others, under some modes of nurture and conditioning of youth than under others. Obviously, there is a great amount of further research required in order to trace more accurately the processes and conditions that affect the standards and values and attitudes of the young as they respond to their life circumstances. The growing boy or girl is subject to influences from a continually changeful system of interactive environments: the physical neighborhood, the home, the circle of acquaintances, the special experiences of the individual, and the pervasive modes of communication that convey the temper of the times and the doings and sufferings of other people. To the complex impact of this system, as particularized in the individual situation, the youth responds according to his innate disposition and his previous conditioning.

It will then be the task of the second part of this report, in reviewing the whole problem of causation, to analyze the evidence back of the different incidences of delinquency in comparable situations, in order to arrive at some conclusions respecting the relative significance of particular control factors. This in turn will lead to Part Three, where we examine the application of such controls to the prevention and to the treatment of delinquency.

We have reached a point at which certain conclusions have become sufficiently clear, as follows:

1. In the high-delinquency areas there are present, to a greater extent than in other areas, environmental conditions and responsive modes and habits of living that in conjunction evoke in youth a sense of frustration, a balking of energies and ambitions, with consequent tendencies to resort to legally forbidden activities by way of substitution or compensation.

2. While a majority of the young in these areas are suffi-

ciently resistant or adaptable to carry on or to find a way to surmount these obstacles, others are more sensitive, more prone to rebelliousness, or more seriously maladjusted to the conditions imposed on them, conditions that even in high-delinquency areas vary considerably in their character and the severity of their impact. It is among the latter group that the *habit* of delinquency is most frequently developed.

3. The *focus* of the clash between youthful wants and aspirations and the resistant conditions is normally the family circle, though influences from the larger environment may stimulate or accentuate it.

4. In lower delinquency areas strains and tensions, again usually focusing in family relations, are for some youth powerful enough to evoke a similar rebelliousness, with a consequent tendency to delinquent behavior.

5. The over-all increase in juvenile delinquency must be attributed to pervasive influences arising from broad changes in the condition of our inclusive civilization. The deep disturbances created by wars and the aftermaths of wars have brought about changes in attitudes, weakening the sense of security and making inroads into our value systems. Directly or indirectly through the effect on parents and elders and through the media of communication, acculturation of the young has been affected. The manner and degree in which this educational change has taken place for different groups and in different countries is a difficult subject for exploration, but we may assume that it has weakened the acceptance of authority, induced more of a skeptical attitude, and made the susceptible more familiar with violence and more inclined to resort to it under stress.

Note on Departmental Approaches to Delinquency

In the preceding section we sketched the approaches of different departments of scholarship to the study of delinquency. There has been controversy over the respective importance of the sociological, the psychological, the psychiatric, the psychoanalytic, and the genetic modes of interpretation. Such controversy, however, is on a minor level, mostly incident to the roles of practitioners of different affiliations in schools and other institutions concerned with delinquents. Sociological classifications of delinquents are usually on a somewhat different basis from psychological ones and quite distinctly different from psychoanalytic ones. All may be equally relevant and equally good, but one can certainly quarrel with the assumption that any one basis is definitive as against the others. As we have been insisting, delinquency is a phenomenon that is the result of the impact of a conjuncture of diverse conditions on susceptible youth. The individual is not merely a sociological or a psychological or somatic being. Any trained investigator should be able to distinguish and report on the environment and the overt symptoms. Any intelligent school teacher should be able to identify the signs of trouble in the pupils under his supervision. Sociologists, psychologists, social psychologists, and anthropologists, out of a common interest in the processes of group formation and cohesion, have all studied the delinquent gang. The report of any such study contains very little to indicate whether it was made by a sociologist, or, say, an anthropologist, except perhaps that either one may use the particular jargon of his school. Differences of interpretation often seem as wide between members of the same discipline—between two anthropologists such as Margaret Mead and Ernest A. Hooten—as between two members of different disciplines. Academic departmental lines are intrusions and embarrassments when the object of study is a many-aspected social phenomenon. They also cause trouble and an unrealistic division of labor in the treatment process, but we shall leave that subject for later consideration.

Part Two

LEADS TO

CAUSATION

4

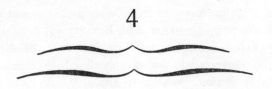

Statement of the Problem

A phenomenon so widespread as juvenile delinquency and one arousing so much public concern and evoking so many agencies and programs to deal with it inevitably leads to numerous explanations. Nearly everyone who comes into contact with it is ready to tell us its cause or causes, as well as what should be done about it. Besides these popular offhand interpretations there are the more responsible contributions of professional researchers. The studies of the latter have been of great service in advancing our understanding of the problem, but there are nevertheless among them various divergent and uncoordinated viewpoints. Since to the educated outsider the whole subject must appear confusing, we begin our discussion with a series of comments aimed at presenting the issue in a proper focus.

The Limits of Causal Inquiry

We do not ask: What is the cause of delinquency? To ask why any delinquency occurs is like asking why human nature is what it is. We are not concerned with the occasional delinquencies in which practically every young person indulges at some time or another. Our interest is in the processes and experiences that lie back of the *habit* of delinquent behavior. Our interest lies not in the act of delinquency but in the delinquent. Nor do we look for an answer that would explain why any individual youth becomes a delinquent. The full investigation of the causation of delinquency in an individual case would mean the most intimate comprehension of his heredity, his mental makeup, his early experiences, his relationships with the family, the school, the playground, the neighborhood—a comprehension that is rarely, if ever, possible to attain. We do have some excellent studies of the history and background of individual delinquents—for example, in Bruno Bettelheim's *Truants From Life*—but, enlightening as these are, we cannot be sure they tell the whole story. Besides, no one life history is the same as any other.

Instead, research into causes must be directed to the discovery of significant relationships between delinquency and other phenomena. We begin by asking for correlations, the concomitance of delinquency with situations or conditions which will show that where delinquency is more prevalent or less prevalent other factors are at the same time more prevalent or less prevalent. We relate the variable of delinquency to other variables and then seek to probe into the association between the concomitant variables, framing hypotheses concerning a possible connection and finding methods of testing them. This statement is of course very obvious. We have much statistical evidence regarding variations in different localities, for different groups, at different times. What we are seeking is the reasons for such variations. As with nearly all causal investigations in the social sciences, the object is to understand why the more or the less: the more here, the less there; the more now, the less then; the more under some specified conditions, the less under others.

On this basis we are confronted with the two major types of questions already mentioned. One—the outstanding question— is how to account for the constantly increasing volume of juvenile delinquency, as evidenced by statistics of police arrests, court adjudications, youthful felonies, institutional commitments, FBI reports on crime and delinquency, and so forth. It is no doubt impossible to discover what proportion of the statistical increase is due to circumstances other than an increase in the actual amount of delinquency—the greater number of reporting agencies, the development of juvenile courts, increased police attention to youthful offenses, greater public concern, and more attention in the press. Since all authorities seem agreed that such adventitious considerations are quite insufficient to explain the recorded increase, as year after year it continues to rise, we have here a most challenging problem.

The second type of question, which has some implication for the first, is addressed to the marked disparity in the incidence of delinquency for different areas, classes, and groups within the community. The study of these differentials is of first importance alike for the understanding and the control of delinquency. Moreover, questions along these lines are fully amenable to direct investigation and have already been pursued with a considerable degree of success, whereas for the first type of question our usual research procedures are of little avail. We are dealing here with broad trends affecting the civilization of our time. We must surmise that growing up in today's world is subject to wide-ranging influences that have an unsettling effect on the mind of our youth, and our conclusions on this theme can hardly admit of total verification.

The Polarities of Causation

The ancient question, how far is heredity responsible and how far environment, is raised in discussions of delinquency as of many other problems. We have been considering the conditions existing in the high-delinquency areas. The areas in question, the slum environment, have certainly some responsibility for the prevalence of delinquency in them. If they were abolished and their residents given decent housing, along with aid in adapting themselves to the new environment, we cannot doubt that delinquency would be reduced. Moreover, since amelioration of living conditions is within the power of the urban authorities, the onus for the prevalence of delinquency must rest with these, and with the citizens who are unwilling to support a campaign for the abolition of the slums. If we say that the residents of the slums are themselves responsible, we are giving a specious excuse for the avoidance of an obligation. If we say that the "bad seed"

is the root of the trouble, we are complacently ignoring the flagrant evidence of the role played by the environmental conditions
on the youth subjected to them.

On the other hand, we cannot hold the unfavorable environment wholly responsible. Large numbers of young persons who
are brought up in the slum environment do not become delinquents. Can we then account for the nondelinquents in the slum
environment by attributing their immunity to better heredity?
Obviously the problem is not so simple. We may find some evidence that the family life of the nondelinquents was on the
whole more stable, that the father or the mother or both took
more care of the children, showed more affection toward them,
exercised more reasonable discipline over them. But the differential behavior of such parents cannot be purely assigned to their
superior stock. They too were bred under particular conditions
and underwent particular experiences. The formative influences
of their upbringing would certainly have something to do with
the manner in which in turn they brought up their own children.
Indoctrinations, social influences of all sorts, and personal experiences mold the native plasticity of the human mentality in
ways beyond the reckoning.

There have been some attempts—as in the study by Healy
and Bronner—to take contrasting pairs of siblings and compare
their respective life histories. Various factors were found to
characterize the delinquents as contrasted with the nondelinquents. In the Healy and Bronner study some 27 per cent of the
delinquents had had many or severe illnesses, as against less
than 8 per cent of the "controls." Some 24 per cent of the delinquents showed neurotic or psychotic deviations; only 2 per cent
of the "controls." Was the difference due to heredity? Hereditary
differences are frequent often in children of the same parents,
since the combinations of genetic elements are always variant.
But environment is also at work. Even the age differential between two children in the same family means a significantly different environment for each.

It should be obvious, then, that we can never demarcate the
precise roles of heredity and environment in determining the

social behavior of the young. The relation of the two is woven from birth, from before birth. There is, for example, significant evidence that stresses and worries affecting the mother during pregnancy can have an adverse effect on the emotional development of her child. There is no assignable beginning. Children inherit from parents and remoter ancestors. All life long we are responsive, in whatever degree, to changing environments. The process is wholly continuous. Moreover, we all help to make our own changing environments, with every decision we take. Heredity and environment are both inconceivably complex, and the union of the two in any individual case is a pattern that shows no seams.

In short, heredity and environment belong to the category of polarities. Life cannot exist or develop without environment, without the particular kind of environment to which the particular kind of life is more or less adapted. Wherever the environment changes, life changes too. Wherever life exists it modifies in some respect its environments. There is this difference, however, that over the relatively short period the living being is the prime mover, the dynamic agent in the more important changes in the relationship. For the strategy of remedial action we should therefore concentrate on producing the desirable environmental change, as in the abolition of slums. While preventive care and remedial treatment are important, so long as these areas of squalor and congestion exist they will continue to breed delinquency.

The Multiplicity of Factors

A major difficulty in arriving at causal connections between delinquency and the phenomena we find to be associated with it is that there are so many phenomena and that they fall into such diverse categories. We can, of course, find out the closeness of the correlation between delinquency and any other particular phenomenon within a given context, but there is often considerable variation in other contexts. Some associated phenomena may be closely correlated because they in turn are correlated with some third phenomenon. We find, say, a close correlation in certain urban areas between the amount of delinquency and the amount of tuberculosis; this may have no direct significance for our purpose, since tuberculosis is most often found in the dilapidated abodes of sheer poverty, a general characteristic of these areas. But the fact that many kinds of sociopathological conditions manifest themselves in these areas may have some significance, since such conditions contribute to the pressures and tensions that promote delinquency. We may learn, to take a finding from Bernard Lander, that areas of Baltimore in which there are large numbers of both whites and Negroes have higher delinquency rates than areas in which one group or the other is a small minority. This correlation may well be significant, but only if it can be related to adverse reactions in the relationship of the two groups under these conditions.

In Part One we reviewed various conditions characteristic of high-delinquency urban areas, on the general assumption that the differential conditions accompanying high delinquency rates are somehow, in some of their aspects, prejudicial to decent law-abiding behavior on the part of the young, tending to breed attitudes conducive to delinquency. We distinguished three broad ranges of such differential conditions: the physical environment of certain urban areas, the socioeconomic milieu of the groups which inhabited such areas, and the mental-emotional characteristics of some of the youth, as distinct from others living in the same area. Within each range variants occurred which affected the correlation with delinquency. For example, a socioeconomic group with a quite distinctive culture—say, a highly orthodox group with continuous and rigorous indoctrination of the young —can inhabit the type of area associated with high delinquency and still not exhibit the delinquency rate characteristic of the area. We also noted that the nearer social circle of the family may be such as to counteract the adverse influences of the neighborhood life or, on the other hand, accentuate their impact.

These illustrations highlight two aspects of the research problem. In the first place, the causal efficacy of any factor or of any complex of environmental factors depends on its relations to other factors or to a complex of conditions existing on a different level. In other words, to comprehend the differential delinquency of any area we must take into account the accommodation between the physical environment and the socioeconomic conditions, along with the cultural background of the inhabitants, and to get closer to the problem we must include also the nearer familial environment of the exposed youth and then the innate and acquired psychic attributes that help us to distinguish delinquents from non-delinquents.

In the second place, we must not think of the causes of delinquency as a series of social forces each of which has its own unit efficacy, greater or less, so that when a sufficient number of them combine they produce a corresponding amount of delinquency. A single factor, or any particular combination of factors, has *by itself* no implications for the causation of delinquency. All the conditions and surroundings of sheer poverty may be present and yet may be remarkably free from delinquent tendencies. It is the *interaction* of conditions as together they bear on some *particular* type of mentality that determines the development of delinquent tendencies. The response that takes the form of habitual delinquency is a manifestation of human nature that is no sense abnormal.

The delinquent attitude is not suddenly evoked by the conjunction of conditions at any one moment, but develops through a series of stages, through the persistence or the successive impact of influences adverse to a law-abiding way of life. The process may be hastened or slowed. It may be hastened by some shock that makes a deep impression on a young person—say, by a punishment the boy regards as wholly unfair, by a special act of brutality on the part of a father, by a sudden realization that the youth is not "wanted," or even by an accident such as a facial disfiguration. Such acts may be said to trigger a tendency, confirming it against counter tendencies, marking the parting of the ways. Any such act may prick through the resistance of youth, and the emotional revulsion contains a new note, a note of defiance—something more than a mere feeling of rebelliousness that subsides when the irritating situation is forgotten. The new note is a vindication of the outraged personality, a repudiation of responsible authority, the recognition of an approaching struggle for new self-assertion, a rift between the youth and his immediate world. The rift will widen into alienation unless some drastic change takes place. On the other hand, a timely release from brooding tensions, a new association, the guidance of some trusted person may effectively reverse a delinquent tendency, and be also a parting of the ways, before it is too late. These considerations suggest the total inadequacy of any interpretation that attributes delinquency to the impact of a single factor or series of "factors."

The Significant Factors

It is unwise, as we have seen, to depend in a causal inquiry on the correlation of factors, or, say, on the number of factors correlated with delinquency in a particular situation. A correlation is for the student a question mark calling for analysis as to its relevance, if any, to a problem. What is specially important, instead, is to look for factors that provide significant leads toward at least a partial solution for the problem.

Among these significant factors must be included those we have designated as "trigger" factors. Let us take, for example, the case of a family where the father and mother are badly at odds. The father is a ne'er-do-well and out of a job; the mother is so beset and hard-worked that she gives little attention to her six children, except in the numbing effort to feed and clothe them. The oldest boy, thirteen, is messy and moody. Because of home pressures he cannot attend to his schooling, for which he is reasonably well qualified. He cherishes a smoldering resentment against it all, but manages to carry on. Then one day the father, finding him in the way, angrily pushes him around. The boy answers back with temper, whereupon the father beats him mercilessly. It is the trigger act. The boy changes direction and his new hatred of authority leads him toward a delinquent career.

Most children are by nature conformists. A long process of disillusionment, the constant beat of balking circumstances, may gradually undermine this tendency. Sometimes, there is a crucial situation that breaks down the defenses; and only then will the various associated conditions—family disorganization, school retardation, destitution—conspire to confirm the attitude that a critical personal experience has evoked. It is the spur to a changed motivation that counts, whether it be a sudden shock to the integrity of the personality, or a series of repeated blows that destroys the resistance weakened by the first, or the persistent pressure of untoward conditions bearing down on a mentality that can no longer endure the weight. Much depends on the youth's own values in relation to the values of his own peer group; much on his innate strength of character in pursuing his resolves; in any event, the turning point from conformity to delinquency will be reached by more young people where adverse conditions are more sustained and more frequent, as in high-delinquency areas.

The concept of the critical factor is often employed in another sense, in which one particular condition is claimed to be the paramount cause of delinquency. Sometimes the condition is so broad that it is nothing less than a bracket for a whole system of conditions—"social disorganization" is an example—and therefore the attribution is unhelpful. A somewhat more specific condition frequently considered paramount is the "broken home." "Broken homes"—that is, homes in which one parent is missing, especially while the children are quite young—figure in the life stories of enough delinquents to indicate that this condition is important. Healy and Bronner, for example, found that out of 4,000 delinquents they identified in Chicago and Boston about 50 per cent came from broken homes.[1] But the broken home usually associated with delinquency is mostly found in high-delinquency areas and suffers from various other conditions adverse to the well-being of the children. It is usually, in other words, a factor in a complex that as a whole is unfavorable to the upbringing of children. Moreover, the fact that the home is broken may itself be explained, in part at least, by the presence of these other adverse conditions. Desertion, for example, is in some neighborhoods a not infrequent occurrence in families already rife with troubles. In a later section, incidentally, we describe a situation in which a home from which the father was missing, seemed to play no part whatever in the evocation of delinquency.

Critical factors are resorted to also for the *prediction* of delinquency, as indicators of a type of disturbance very often associated with habitual delinquency. In this type of approach there is danger of confusing two senses of the term "prediction." It may refer to an overt or easily discernible aspect of the condition it identifies, as, for example, a particular kind of rash indicates a particular type of disease; or it may refer to a signal, or harbinger, or concomitant of a phenomenon of which the indicator is not an aspect nor in any way a determinant. Many of our popular weather indicators are of the latter type. When the gulls fly over the land, it is supposed to indicate a storm; when the sunrise is red, it is the "shepherd's" warning. Some of the proposed indicators of delinquency take the form of a rather elaborate scale, consisting presumably of actual determinants. The well-known Glueck prediction scale falls in this category.

The factors designated by the Gluecks for this purpose are a series of interfamily relationships: the role played by the father in maintaining discipline, the mother's supervision, the affection for the child shown by each parent, and the cohesiveness of the family group. This scale has occasioned much discussion, mostly critical. Some serious technical defects have been pointed out, and the significance of the percentages of accuracy claimed has been correctly challenged. We do not regard any scale of this type as particularly useful for purposes of prediction. The factors are usually not clear-cut. In the Glueck scale they sum up to little more than one—family cohesiveness—which is itself a whole system of relationships, and no easier to assess than the more obvious signs of disturbance in a child. Such cohesiveness depends on many conditions, some of which certainly lie outside of the family circle. The great importance of the family life is very properly stressed by the Gluecks. But many forces from the environment impinge on the life of the family and have their significant share in making it what it is. It has been suggested that for multiproblem families the causes of their trouble lie more within than outside the family, but this too is a quite dubious proposition.

There is still another sense in which we may speak of critical factors. Of the multitude of conditions associated with a relatively high incidence of delinquency, some are so bound up with others that they cannot be regarded as independent correlates; some may be incidental; some may be merely consequential; and some may be products of the same complex of conditions from which delinquency arises. Through statistical devices we can in a measure determine which of various correlated factors are clearer indications of the presence of delinquency, and which are better indicators of the delinquency rate.

An illustration offered is in Bernard Lander's *Towards an Understanding of Juvenile Delinquency* (Columbia University Press, 1942). He concluded that in a mixed area the percentage of non-whites and the percentage of home ownership were indicators almost as effective as a much larger number of variables taken together. Where the percentage of home ownership was relatively high, delinquency rates were low. This conclusion was for the city of Baltimore and could not be generalized without similar research in different types of cities. More broadly, Lander concluded that two clusters of characteristics sufficed to account for almost all the covariation of factors, these being "socioeconomic status," referring to factors indicating educational level and housing conditions, and "anomie" (his term for far-reaching social disorganization) correlated with the percentages of Negro population and those of home ownership and delinquency itself. His most drastic inference was that low economic status was not significantly related to delinquency unless it was accompanied by the demographic factors spelling "anomie." Lander's study aroused considerable interest and some constructively critical comments.[2] He is now engaged in a follow-up study of larger scale, covering Baltimore and two other cities in different parts of the country, in which he plans to include several additional factors for the determination of the presence of "anomie."

To conclude, the statistical study of the correlations of delinquency with a variety of other conditions or factors can take us only a part of the way to understanding of the causation of delinquency. We shall see later in Part Two that any particular area of the environment of youth—the home, the school, the playground, the street—may be the focus or the spur of the kind of disturbance and disorientation that is likely to result in delinquency. The young grow up with a set of expectations and aspirations that are relative both to their indoctrinations and to the situations within which they are bred, and the conditions that defeat these expectations and aspirations vary accordingly. Delinquency is the similar response of disgruntled or defeated youth to a particular collocation of circumstances that provoke deep-seated resentments and rebellion. Always we must get down to the impact of conditions on the mind of youth. The *motivation* of delinquency must be understandable before the quest for causation can end.

Influences emanating from the outside, adverse conditions of the locality, thwartings and maladjustments in the home, school frustrations, unhappy associations, untoward circumstances of any sort—except so far as they are counteracted by constructive influences, together make their impact on the minds of the young, who in turn respond according to their particular capacities and limitations. Experience alone can teach us which conjunctures of conditions in varying environments are most prejudicial to the development of a well-ordered life for the growing child. Already we have sufficient evidence to enable us to use this experience far more effectively than it has been as yet, both for preventing and for checking delinquent tendencies. This evidence is the basis for the strategy considerations we develop in Part Three.

Causation and Treatment

In our judgment a decided weakness in many of the programs, not least the official programs, directed to the treatment of delinquents is the fact that they are not geared to the on-going researches of various kinds—sociological, psychological, and psychiatric—that are increasingly throwing light on the nature and problem of delinquent behavior. Treatment programs are too often not armed with the skills needed to cope with the difficult task of rehabilitation. We point out elsewhere the great need for better screening of cases, for better understanding of the problems of the young, for special attention to the early stages of trouble. It has been too often assumed that the treatment of delinquents is a matter of common sense, or good will, or proper discipline, and very few attempts have been made to test the assumption by a follow-up of the treatment. But such inadequate records as we possess indicate that the results are far from satisfactory.

It is sometimes asserted that study of the causation of delinquency does not provide solutions to the problems of prevention and of reform; that such solutions are more likely to be found through experience on the job, through trial and error; that the cure of a disease is often found when the cause is still unknown. The last statement, however, is at best incomplete and may be quite misleading. In some areas, including medicine, cures or solutions of problems have been discovered even where the specific causal connection is unknown. The discovery of various antibiotic drugs is an illustration. But such discoveries were preceded by research that revealed the role of viruses in the causation of disease and the counteracting effects of various bacterial agencies. In medicine vast efforts are devoted to the etiology of disease, and in cancer and heart disease, for example, with already significant results. The chances of the discovery of a cure are immensely advanced if we can reach down to the causative factors. Even an intermediate link in the causal chain can be most important for treatment or prevention. Such was the discovery of the relationship between malaria and the anopheles mosquito.

What is especially important for treatment is the study of the background of the delinquent. We must learn, on the one hand, his previous experiences: his relationships at home; the difficulties, thwartings, misadventures he has met at home, at school, with his associates; the influences that have worked on him; and, on the other hand, the characteristic attitudes he has developed under these conditions, his rationalizations of his behavior, his outlook on life. From this knowledge we can broadly place him in some category, and we have already enough information from research and experience to appreciate what are the most hopeful approaches to a program of treatment. Research is constantly revealing the interrelations and interdependences of conditions —in other words, the causal connections between them. In the light of this knowledge, in the spread of this knowledge, lies our best hope for more effective treatment and more well-grounded efforts toward prevention—especially prevention of the development of those early tendencies that may ripen into confirmed delinquency.

5

Social-Class Theories
of Delinquency

The greater prevalence of youthful delinquency in the poorer urban areas has long been made a subject for study and interpretation. Some earlier studies, such as those of the Chicago school of "social ecologists" and especially of Shaw and McKay,[1] laid stress on the relationship of delinquency to the physical environment and produced statistical evidence to show that the areas of highest delinquency were those transitional areas in which industry was encroaching on residential districts and housing was becoming dilapidated. The successive groups which occupied such deteriorating areas were alike characterized by high delinquency rates. It is noteworthy that each of these successive groups were bodies of in-migrants, entering at a very low economic level. Later studies pointed out some other characteristics of areas in which high delinquency rates prevailed; such was the case, for example, where disprivileged groups, notably Negroes, had made an initial entry into congested districts and met with resistance from the earlier residents.

Other scholars were more concerned with the association between the prevalence of delinquency and the social or class level. In their well-known "Yankee City" studies, Warner and Lunt dwelt upon the association of high delinquency with lower social class.[2] They defined the class level by a composite index, including occupational status, place of residence, educational back-

ground, and housing conditions. The basis of classification is not
wholly satisfactory. It may serve reasonably well as a general
indicator of social class differentials, but it is inadequate as a
criterion of delinquency ratings. We suggest that the two factors
which in combination are most closely associated with delinquency are urbanized poverty and ethnic or racial discrimination. The grounds for this conclusion have already been stated
and will be further developed as we proceed. Such other factors
as occupational status, educational standards, type and place of
residence are mostly consequential on these two.

Other formulations attribute the prevalence of delinquency
to the impact of the prevailing value system of a total society,
the beliefs and practices that are operative, if not openly ac-
knowledged, within it. The young are attuned to follow the example set by their elders and those who are more limited in
their opportunities or less competent in evasion get into trouble,
though they may be no more delinquent than, say, the shrewd
officials of a big corporation who succeed in flouting the legal
code. This is the position taken by writers like Milton Barron.[3]
The view that children imitate the ways of the fathers is of
course an old and reasonably respectable sociological doctrine.
It is broadly acceptable, but quite inadequate to explain the
varieties of behavior or the changing values of successive generations. The growing youth is exposed to conflicting or competing
values, and often enough is resistant to or restive under some
of the indoctrinations of his breeding. The theory fails to take
into account the impact of differential environments and of
changing situations on the young, for in one important sense the
environment of every group is different and the situation of
every new generation differs from that of its predecessor. The
theory is too wholesale, and entirely lacking in subtlety.

Within the same general context two recent theories call for
more detailed examination, since they are sponsored by highly
competent students of the subject and contain some important
insights. The differences between the two are also significant.
Albert K. Cohen[4] maintains that the high delinquency rate is
largely due to the baffled aspiration of lower-class youth to rise

to middle-class status; whereas, according to Walter B. Miller, the lower-class culture spontaneously generates among its young a "delinquent subculture."[5] These positions are reminiscent of the viewpoint of the Chicago "ecologists" who held that the character of the urban area in which lower-class youth were bred put pressures on them which explained the higher delinquency rate.

Cohen, the leader in this newer line of interpretation, holds that lower-class youth are caught in a vise between the way of living and the philosophy of life characteristic of their own class and the influences exerted by the middle-class conditions and attitudes to which they are in one way or another exposed. They lack the means, the habituations, and the training to realize their aspirations to this higher status. The values current in their own class—the easy spending of whatever they make, the lack of industriousness, the uncalculating aggressiveness of manner—are contrary to typical middle-class ways. Frustrated in their ambitions they fall back with a kind of revulsion to the values of their own class. They react with hostility to "middle-class norms" and to the assumptions of superiority of middle-class youth. Cohen regards a certain wanton and aimless brutality exhibited by some delinquents as a violent repudiation of middle-class standards. They seek for status in illegitimate ways, ganging up to assert their own internal status.

Some features of Cohen's theory are certainly significant and give a lead to further advances in the interpretation of delinquent behavior. He emphasizes the effect of frustration, of baffled aspiration, of the falling back on illegitimate means to enhance the quest for status within a peer group in an unpropitious environment. He provides good insights and fine descriptions concerning the undirected or nonutilitarian character of youthful gang behavior, which is in marked contrast to the operation of the adult gang. Various students of the subject have followed and developed Cohen's viewpoint. Cloward and Ohlin have recognized that youth subject to the stresses and lacks emphasized by Cohen may react in a variety of ways, in response to different situations or "opportunity structures," and specify three particular reactions.[6] The first or criminal-minded type seeks illegitimate means and devious associations for immediate profit, hoping to make a killing. The second, the conflict gang, corresponds to Cohen's group, concerned with "rep"—status attained through fights and toughness. The third is the withdrawn or "retreatist" type, shuffling along for the snatched pleasures of the moment, getting by and keeping out of trouble when they can, and resorting to escapist devices, dope and drink and sexual indulgences. Another line of classification of the types of deviant behavior has been proposed by Robert K. Merton.[7] Most relevant here is what he styles "behavioral ritualism" in which the deviant, rejecting some aspects of his social milieu and overconforming to others that fit in with his interests, retreats, along with fellow deviants, into special institutionalized activities adapted to the lesser rewards available to him.

Walter B. Miller's interpretation of the role of lower-class culture in the evocation of delinquent behavior is in one respect diametrically opposed to Cohen's. For Miller it is not the baffled aspiration to middle-class status that sparks the retreat into a delinquent subculture; instead, the lower-class culture spontaneously generates the delinquent type in two closely related forms, the adolescent street-corner group as portrayed by William F. Whyte in *Street Corner Society* and the more aggressive law-violating gang. Such delinquency is regarded as primarily an unlawful way of achieving lower-class values. The delinquent subcultures are geared to the "focal concerns" of lower-class life.

The focal concerns specified are trouble, toughness, excitement, belonging, status, fate, autonomy. This congeries of preoccupations strikes us as a curious and rather capricious selection, especially when presented as characterizing a particular social class. Miller speaks of them as issues which command widespread or persistent attention and a high degree of emotional involvement, much more than they do in the middle-class society. Why not, to try another selection, economic security, good jobs, a woman at his service, better living conditions, children that grow up to support their parents?

Miller goes on to explain how these focal concerns, especially status and belonging, are built into the behavior system of the young and are given a special direction within the delinquent gang.

The first concern mentioned, trouble, is highly ambivalent in his formulation. It has a different significance for men, women, and children respectively. They all want to keep out of trouble, especially with officials or authorities. But under certain conditions there is also a certain status-conferring distinction in getting into trouble. This prestige element is cultivated in the system of the gang.

We do not feel it is necessary to enlarge on the problems posed by Miller's theory, especially as much of our critique of Cohen is also relevant here. We find much merit in Miller's description of the pressures and impulses that operate in the gang setting. But his descriptions of lower-class concerns are highly selective and needlessly generalized, and the contrasts he finds between the dominant standards of lower-class and of middle-class society are overdrawn and inadequately corroborated. He makes excessive play of some features that may be found sporadically but by no means universally in lower-class society. For example, he dwells considerably on the "female-based" household of lower-class society. It is true that in high-delinquency areas the family is not infrequently broken, or the father out of work or inadequate. But in some of these areas the family is, broadly speaking, patriarchal rather than matriarchal. This is usually the case in Italian sectors and to some extent among Puerto Ricans. As for the contrast with middle-class society, might we not with at least equal plausibility call the middle-class suburban family "female-based" since the father commutes to the city and returns in the evening, sometimes carrying the load of his office into his home and hoping that the mother has settled the problem of the children for the day?

Various aspects of the theories associated with Miller and Cohen have been subjected to an effective critique by a number of sociologists.[8] While these theories have been stimulating and provocative of further research and while they have certainly directed attention to a very significant feature of delinquency problems—the baffled urge of youth for recognition, belonging, status, we hold that they without warrant attribute this feature to the "culture" or the "mobility" or to the low estate of a particular social class. It is with this casual imputation that we are mainly concerned here. In the first place, we find the categories "lower-class culture" and "middle-class culture" somewhat misleading, when used to contrast two different ways of life. In lower- or working-class neighborhoods the amount of recorded delinquency is certainly higher than in more prosperous areas. But there is quite considerable variation among lower-class neighborhoods in amount of delinquency. While studying some tables reporting indices of economic and social conditions in New York City, the writer was struck by the seemingly anomalous position of one Health Center district in Manhattan. Its socioeconomic rating was the third lowest of all the thirty Health Center districts of the City, but its delinquency rating was in the median range and in our indices of social pathology it was also far superior to the high-delinquency areas.

When, however, we examined the figures for ethnic origins in the various districts this particular one proved to have quite a low proportion of recent in-migrants, who consist mainly of Puerto Ricans and Southern Negroes. This finding is entirely in accord with the evidences we present in the text which show that in interpreting delinquency differentials we must look at the specific conjuncture of environmental and demographic factors characterizing a particular area, and not rely on broad and elusive distinctions such as that between lower-class and middle-class culture.[9]

Cohen makes much of the statistical fact that the police and court records show a preponderance of cases occurring in the lower-class areas, but, as we have already pointed out, the statistics are unduly unfavorable to the people of these areas. If, as we have argued, the actual volume of delinquency should be represented as a gradient as we pass from the groups least affected to those with the heaviest incidence, the ground for any identification of delinquency as a class phenomenon is removed. Delinquency occurs in every area, among the youth of every social class, to an extent sufficient to refute the charge that it stems from the "culture" peculiar to a lower social class. If it occurs in greater volume in many lower-class areas there are conditions which cannot properly be called "cultural" that predispose to it. Cohen cites as supporting his thesis a study made by W. C. Kvaraceus. Kvaraceus has certainly shown a strong bias toward Cohen's position but from the study in question we draw a different conclusion. What the "overwhelming majority" of families of delinquent children have in common, said Kvaraceus, is poverty. While there may be some exaggeration in this statement, the association of poverty with higher delinquency rates seems beyond doubt. Is poverty then a cultural attribute? It is not a condition preferred or desired by the poor; quite the contrary. They are habituated to living in poverty and must adjust their behavior to that condition. Because of this necessity, certain culture traits develop, but these do not constitute their culture or even constitute its major characteristics. Even if they did, they still would not necessarily imply any special proneness to delinquency. The earth is still inhabited mostly by poverty-stricken peoples, but we have no grounds for saying that most of them show high delinquency rates. It is where poverty is accompanied by various special conditions, for which the poor cannot possibly be regarded as chiefly responsible, that high delinquency rates prevail.

Delinquency is highest in the deteriorating and overcrowded areas into which in-migrant groups, generally subject to some form of ethnic or racial discrimination, have penetrated, causing a shifting of some part of the earlier populations. The in-migrant groups usually come from more rural areas, are not well adjusted to urban living, arrive without resources or special skills, and during the first generation after their arrival are particularly helpless in alien surroundings and are subject to various forms of exploitation. They have delinquency rates out of proportion to the rest of the population. To attribute their swelling delinquency statistics to the vain efforts of the young to achieve middle-class status does not provide any adequate explanation. There may be no cited evidence of high delinquency in their previous culture—that of the Puerto Ricans is an example. We must therefore find the answer in the conjuncture of unfavorable conditions. It would be a needlessly roundabout conclusion to call the discontent and frustration of the young under these conditions a revulsion, a "reaction formation," resulting from their failure to attain "middle-class status."

It was in the kind of in-migrant area we have just described, in a district of Boston, that Miller made the studies on which he based his theory, and he himself has admitted that his description mainly applied to such "residual lower-class groups." But this limitation surely disqualifies the attribution of certain delinquency traits to a lower class as such, to its "culture," or even to an aspect of its culture. The youth of these impoverished in-migrant groups thrust into urban slums suffer in a particularly high degree from a complex of adverse factors, in their home life, in their schooling, in the pressures of their whole environment. Their expectations, stimulated by the influences deriving from the ambient American environment with its emphasis on "getting on," "rising in the world," even beyond the youthful aspirations characteristic of young people everywhere, are frustrated. The resulting response varies according to the particular youth's temperament, training, or special situation; it may be a kind of resignation, a defiant repudiation of the values that cannot be achieved, a makeshift acceptance of lesser opportunities, a belligerent struggle against what is deemed gross discrimination or neglect or abuse—the variations are endless.

In reacting in any of these ways, these young people—allowing for the difference in the mode of expression—are only doing what youth of any class do when their ambitions or expectations are continuously thwarted and they find themselves thoroughly disgruntled with the conditions that defeat them. The ensuing disorientation or alienation may stem from many different situations and may express itself in many different forms. It may be traceable primarily to excessive or arbitrary discipline or to lack of discipline, to family neglect or mistreatment, to a feeling that one does not belong, to persistent failure of any kind, or even to sheer accident. Delinquency exists in all social classes, and is statistically most prevalent where conditions are such as to evoke attitudes of rebellion, defiance, or, broadly speaking, alienation in a larger proportion of the youthful population. There can be little doubt that the in-migrant groups of ethnic minorities are those most exposed to such conditions.

Under these conditions many youth feel frustrated, certainly, and some of them resort to illegitimate means to relieve their frustration. But their frustration is more directly explained when one learns how and why they are retarded in school, how they feel cramped in the promiscuous environment of one-room or two-room homes and are often at odds with parents who are too ignorant to help them or to understand their problems and who themselves are often bewildered by their own troubles, and when we realize that they have exchanged the congenial friendly neighborliness of the poor communities from which they migrated for the distracting confusion of an urban slum.

Within the urban community the youth of the poor and the youth of the middle class have not such different viewpoints, standards, and aspirations as to create a cultural gulf between them. In the city the neighborhood sense is weakened by mobility, by the mixed character of most neighborhoods, by the many channeled influences of the city as a whole. But the poorer youth read pretty much the same school texts as do those of the middle class; they are taught the same American history; they are subjected to the same American traditions and frequently enough are ready to absorb them. They like pretty much the same comics, watch the same TV programs, and go more or less to the same movies. They have the same love of the same games and they have similar youthful yearnings, similar stirrings and misgivings about sex, though the differences of situation make some differences in resulting relationships. The youth of the middle class gang up in groups and go in for mischievous pranks that not infrequently contain an element of delinquency. They have, however, better life-chances, since their parents have more means to provide these. Their mode of life consequently diverges from that of lower-class youth. The aspirations of middle-class adolescents become geared, most likely, to social

rewards and material success, and in the process of seeking
these their habits and outlooks become increasingly different
from those of that portion of the lower class who live in the
slum areas. Another consideration is that these areas tend to
harbor down-and-outs, misfits, and such resourceless persons.
Adult crime is more frequent than it is in more well-to-do neighborhoods, and the example is more easily followed by susceptible and frustrated youth.

These are broad considerations, but more specific evidences
also discredit the attribution of delinquency to some inclusive
culture complex characteristic of the lower-status society as
such. Some significant statistical evidences, for example, are
offered in a recent study by Reiss and Rhodes,[10] on the basis
of which the authors conclude that "there is no simple relationship between ascribed social status and delinquency." One of
their findings is that the low-status boy who lives in a high-status
area has "almost no chance of becoming a delinquent,"—less
chance, indeed, than the high-status boy of the area. "The more
the lower-class boy is in a minority in the school and residential
community, the less likely is he to become a delinquent." On
the other hand, a high-status boy living in a low-status area has
a greater chance of becoming delinquent than his fellow living
in a high-status area. Such findings would certainly seem to
conflict with the Cohen doctrine that the pressure of middle-
class norms on lower-class boys accounts for their high delinquency rates.

What further inferences can we draw from these and other
corroborative findings? Obviously they illustrate the influence of
an environment on the behavior of those exposed to it. But they
also strongly imply that certain features of an environment are
peculiarly significant for the morale of the young. In the higher-
status environment the low-status youth still lives with his lower-
status family and we have some evidence that suggests he con-
sorts with his status peers in the area. Is his lowered delinquency
rate then to be attributed to the greater opportunities and outlets for his energies that a higher-status neighborhood affords?
Is it because he goes to the same schools and shares the same

social occasions with higher-status youth and thus is encouraged to maintain aspirations for the future that certain conditions of low-status neighborhoods discourage? There are various possibilities here that call for further exploration.

To attribute a particular phenomenon within a social area to its "culture" seems to us to be in any event a quite dubious and unenlightening assertion. In the first place, the term "culture" is a kind of total bracket for all the manifestations of a society, including the phenomena in question. Many sociologists refuse to draw any distinction between a "culture" and a "social system," and those who seek to differentiate them have not succeeded in gaining any wide acceptance. Aside from that, the phenomenon in question, delinquency, cannot be regarded as a norm of the culture, since the majority of young persons within it are not classified as delinquents. At most, we could assume only that the lower-class culture made the young somewhat more exposed or susceptible to delinquent tendencies, and even that assumption must be qualified, since the lower-class group is not responsible for the physical environment and we know that the environmental conditions of overcrowding and consequent promiscuity, as well as the lack of opportunities, must share the blame. Finally, Cohen's explanation for the resort of the low-status group to gang delinquency—that it has in some degree accepted and "internalized" middle-class standards—seems unnecessary in view of all the frustrations that beset the young in getting along in urban slum environments of our great cities, in getting along at school or with their disturbed or disrupted families, in seeking employment, in fulfilling the normal aspirations of boys of any class.

6

Conclusions on the Relation of Culture and Delinquency

We have seen that a number of variant theories have recently been developed which have broadly attributed the prevalence of delinquency, in general or in particular social areas, to the prevailing "culture," in effect to the society itself. The values or goals acceptable to the culture or the social milieu are such, it is claimed, as to be directly or indirectly evocative of delinquency in the young. Of course all behavior of any kind within a society can be attributed to the character of that society. It is then equally responsible for the nondelinquency of the great majority as for the delinquency of the minority. What explains everything explains nothing. We may select certain broad aspects of a society or a culture and conclude that these are favorable to the development of delinquent tendencies. We may take, for example, the mobility characteristic of American life, whether geographical or social ("vertical"), or the plurality of moral and religious codes, or the "loosening of family ties," or the emphasis on financial success, or the prevalence on TV broadcasts of scenes exhibiting crime and violence, or all of these together. We may be justified in regarding these conditions as predisposing to delinquent attitudes, but even so there are multitudes of young persons who do not appear to be seriously affected by them, and moreover, we have to set against such factors those that may on the other hand be conducive to the inculcation of decent citizenship.

In short, what we must know to interpret the incidence and the volume of delinquency, and certainly in order to combat it effectively, is, first, the differential conditions of the narrower areas where the delinquency rate is highest and then the further differentials that apply to the youth in these areas who actually exhibit delinquent habits. These further differentials are the family relations, the school relations, and the neighborhood relations of the affected youth. With these leads we reach finally the particular mentality of the youths themselves—their temperaments, their emotional make-ups, their psychological traits, as these respond to the special predisposing conditions of their new environment and its particular setting for themselves. We will still be far from the full knowledge of why any individual youngster became delinquent while others, perhaps his own siblings, did not, but we will possess reasonably adequate information as to why so many of these youngsters did take to delinquent ways.

The present tendency to attribute the prevalence of delinquency to the impact of the whole "culture" of a society or of a particular class or group is so widespread that some further comments on it may be in order, especially since it often carries the implication that only by wholesale reformation of our value system can we do much about preventing delinquency or reducing its volume.

We question particularly the sharp demarcation of a lower-class value system (or morality or culture) from that generally accepted or pursued by other classes within the total community, and the concomitant stress on the exceptional amount of delinquency it is presumed to engender. We dispute the further assumption that there is a homogeneous lower-class culture or morality, characteristic of all sorts and conditions of people who may be assigned to this lower class.

Let us examine these counts in turn. Walter B. Miller speaks of a "lower-class culture" as a cultural system in its own right, with an integrity of its own, with a characteristic set of practices, focal concerns, and ways of behaving that are meaningfully and systematically related to one another rather than to corresponding features of middle-class culture.[1] We have already disputed the relevance to lower-class culture of the rather curious list of "focal concerns" he assigns to it. The lower class, meaning the class distinguished particularly by its low income level, is not homogeneous. Its delinquency rate varies markedly according to the environmental conditions in which its members are placed. Lower-class residents in small towns in New England and in the West, in some mining villages, in certain urban pockets do not, on any evidence we have, exhibit delinquency rates approaching those of, say, Bedford-Stuyvesant or central Harlem in New York City. Lower-class in-migrants to urban slums exhibit higher delinquency rates than the same groups did prior to this migration. Different environments have a significant relation to life chances and to attitudes. The youths of groups subject to discrimination usually have inferior educational advantages and career opportunities. We have no reason to assume that the lower class is inherently less law-abiding than any higher class. The response to the denial of opportunities, taking the form of rebelliousness and resort to illegitimate means, is a natural human response not limited to any class.

One of the disadvantages of the unduly sharp demarcation of cultural or social lines is that it prevents a proper estimation of the differences that do distinguish groups—income groups, class groups, religious groups, ethnic groups, and all others. Differences exist everywhere within an area of common living, and so do likenesses. Difference and likeness combine in endless ways, creating congenialities and aversions of every description. The more insulated or exclusive a group is, the greater will be its characteristic differences from those of the environing community. Under some conditions, where seclusion from the rest of society is marked or complete, we may properly speak of a subculture. A ghetto becomes a subculture in time, as does a certain type of monastery, or a prison for criminals with lengthy sentences. But the term is not appropriate to a social class which is exposed to the same kind of schooling, the same media of communication, and numerous other forms of contact within the one larger society.

We turn to our second count. The delinquency recorded against lower-class youth is not different in kind but only in degree from that in higher economic groups; in fact we have sufficient reason to believe that official statistics tend to overestimate the disparity between lower and higher economic groups in the prevalence of delinquency. We have already offered some evidence tending to discount the sharper differentials of the official statistics, but a further illustration may be given here. One study, covering a rather large sample of Western and Midwestern high-school-age youth and using a measure of reported delinquent behavior instead of the official figures of police and courts, actually found no significant differences in the amount of delinquency of boys and girls of different socioeconomic levels.[2] We cannot doubt that the actual volume of delinquency is greater under certain circumstances, as in our great cities, for some markedly disadvantaged lower-class groups, but there too we have reason to believe that the differential is not nearly as steep as the official figures indicate. We must definitely reject Miller's thesis that "lower-class culture" has its own value system that predisposes its youth toward delinquency in a quite special way.

We cannot regard the delinquency figures for various city slum areas as an indication that there is a homogeneous lower-class culture. We cannot accept the view that a lower economic class exhibits motivations and aspirations distinctively different from those of the more prosperous classes. All want the same kinds of things within the limits of their respective circumstances. These bloc theories of culture exaggerate differences that are more attributable to differential environment than to inbred differences of values. If we want to get to grips with the problem of youthful delinquency we must think instead of eliminating slum conditions with their concomitant disadvantages and handicaps of the young, and meanwhile of providing aid, direction, and opportunity for the more vulnerable youth of such areas before delinquency habits are formed or confirmed.

Delinquency as the Repudiation of Culture

The subjective and insecure grounds of the culture-bound theories of delinquency may perhaps be inferred from the fact that the two leading exponents whose views we have been examining offer quite contradictory interpretations of it. For Cohen it is not the lower class itself that breeds delinquent tendencies but the unsuccessful attempt to pass beyond it, to rise out of it into middle-class society and its contrasting culture. For Miller, on the other hand, it is within the lower-class culture that delinquency is fostered, by the very nature of its "focal concerns."

Alongside of these doctrines we may place the view that confirmed delinquency implies a total rejection of the values sustaining the society. These values are not those of any particular group, but of the society as a whole. Thou shalt not rob, thou shalt not damage the property of thy neighbor, and so forth. These injunctions are not the code of a group; they are fundamental prescriptions common to civilized society. The confirmed delinquent rejects them. In other words, he puts himself outside the code. He is at odds with society. He is in a state of "anomie," a term first popularized by the French sociologist, Emile Durkheim, to signify rulelessness.

We have seen that a characteristic attitude associated with habitual delinquency is a sense of frustration, rebellion, alienation—alienation from the ways of the home, from the requirements of the school, from the prescriptions of authorities who intervene to punish the delinquents or to try to reform them. They add at odds with their society. "Anomie," however, is too strong a term to express accurately their state of mind. They break laws without compunction (many "respectable" people do the same when they can get away with it safely), and they go further in exhibiting a dislike and hatred of authority, disregarding obligations which the large majority of the young respect. But there are limits to their lawlessness. They observe some rules, and in their gangs they follow a rather strict code of their own, with its appropriate loyalties.

Robert Merton has accordingly described the attitude as "modified anomie," a condition in which culturally prescribed goals are pursued by "anomic" means, illegitimate because either unlawful or morally taboo. The characterization is neat and the term "modified anomie" might be acceptable, but the reference to "culturally prescribed goals" may be misleading. Are the ends sought by the habitual delinquent properly designated as culturally prescribed, and if so, in what sense? Is it the ends or the means that are culturally prescribed? The ends delinquents usually pursue are simple ends, ends that youth everywhere seek, irrespective of particular cultures. They want more liberty, less control by elders or authorities, more recognition, more affection, more congenial peer associations, certain material objects within reach but which they can attain only by filching, certain pleasures, such as riding in cars, which they miss but are tempted to seize illegally. Some of these ends they seek to gain by illegitimate means, others by setting up their own organizations in order to obtain within them a substitute for the recognition, status, and freedom otherwise denied them.

Moreover, the means they employ, whether illegitimate or legitimate, are not calculated or intended to secure what we usually think of as specifically cultural ends. We think of American culture as geared to success, to rising in the world through the acquisition of wealth, to the entrance of the young into colleges and universities which open the road to higher status—in general, to material prosperity. But delinquents only exceptionally pursue these goals. The illegitimate means they adopt are sporadic and undirected to any end beyond an immediate gratification. Their petty filching is mostly bravado, prank, something to show the others, an incidental response to easy opportunity. Their rowdyism gets them nowhere except into trouble. The only regularized resort to illegitimate means, if we except the minority case of the narcotic addict, is to de-

fend, in the name of status, a most unprofitable claim. It is the
gang's defense of its "turf" against the invasion of the members
of another gang, leading to "rumbles" with their danger to life
and limb and the likelihood of police arrest. Such illegitimate
activities are no more designed to advance a career than are
the legitimate contests of schoolboy athletics.

The lack of "access to legitimate means" is made much of in
some recent theories of delinquency, and this obvious feature of
slum life is certainly provocative of delinquency. But the effect
is not designed to remove the cause. Poverty, the peculiarly
cramping poverty of the city slum, is a major reason why slum
youth cannot compete effectively with the youth of better neighborhoods in the scramble for the "good things of life"—poverty
as a lack of capital for enterprise, but, even more, poverty as
blocking in multiple ways the educational and social preparation
well-to-do youths enjoy, poverty as debarring slum youths from
the associations the well-to-do possess with influential persons
who give them promising jobs, poverty as inculcating certain
modes of speech, mannerisms, and habits that are taboo in
higher economic circles. No illegitimate means available to the
disprivileged youth can serve as a substitute for the means they
lack. The illegitimate means to which they resort are no equivalent, bring no comparable rewards; they are at best an unhappy
makeshift, a very partial release from the frustrations they feel.
Only in so far as society reforms the conditions and makes ac-
cessible the legitimate means, will these youths be able effectively
to pursue "culturally prescribed goals."

Salient and Crucial Situations in the Causation of Delinquency

We have referred to certain "trigger" events that can mean the parting of the ways, decisive occasions that upset the uneasy or unstable equilibrium of a youth who up to that point has been "going straight," though subjected to strains or harassing restrictions or failures. Such an event may be, for example, a jarring rebuff, some treatment that seems to the youth grossly unfair, the loss of a mother in a time of trouble, or personal disfigurement resulting from an accident or a disease such as acne. Prominent among such precipitating situations are happenings that mean a loss of "face," the realization that one has been rejected or does not belong with peers or within the family circle. The "outcast" feeling especially is the kind of disorienting experience that leads to confirmed delinquency.

The crucial situation may not be a single event but the climax of a series of frustrations or disappointments, the breaking point before the turning point. An instance of this is offered sometimes when a boy who has been doing poorly at school and behaving not too well otherwise becomes definitely a school drop-out. The die is cast, and the new situation makes easy the road to confirmed delinquency.

We have spoken of the crucial situation as precipitating the downward turn, but we should recognize also that a timely intervention may mean a turnabout in the opposite direction. A wise counselor at the right moment, a bit of friendly aid in a time of trouble, a considerate parent who honestly probes to the root of a misunderstanding between himself and his boy, may inaugurate a change of outlook that can lead to a new direction of behavior. There are many vulnerable youth, suffering disturbances and tendencies beset by grudges and fears, whose future depends on what is done to them and for them at this crucial stage. Here, indeed, is the greatest field for preventive treatment against the development of delinquency.

In the following paragraphs we characterize certain ways in which, within the major areas of youthful experience, critical or crucial situations develop.

The Family Circle

Since the family is the primary and almost universal locus for the upbringing of the young, there is naturally a large amount of literature dealing with its role in that respect. In a very broad sense it might be claimed that any serious tendency to delinquency in the young can be attributed to family upbringing, but only in the sense in which the development of all kinds of tendencies, for better or worse, are at least to a degree dependent on what happens in the family. We shall here endeavor merely to indicate certain critical situations in family relationships that may determine whether a particular child goes straight or develops attitudes conducive to delinquency.

There are various family conditions that are repeatedly the source of delinquent behavior. We hear much, for example, of "broken homes," and the records of institutions for delinquents frequently show a disproportionate number of children who come from such homes. No doubt a broken home, with only one parent to aid and guide and support the children, can be quite detrimental to a child's welfare, but we must remember that the youthful inmates of institutions come mostly from homes which have other serious defects. Desertion is not infrequently the cause of a broken home, and it by no means follows that the presence of the kind of father who is ready to abandon his family obligations bodes any good to the children. The charge is sometimes made that the children of working mothers are more liable to become delinquent, but various studies have shown little or no basis for it.

What is of much greater importance in the upbringing of children is the type of relationship established in the earliest years between parents and children. The first learning, the first contacts with what we call reality, the first indoctrinations come from the parents. The actual content of what is instilled and the viewpoints concerning people or the meaning of things, are very often dissolved in the process of growing up, by subsequent experiences and by what the child learns at school, from the media of communication, and from the give-and-take of social contacts. What endures much more firmly, striking more deeply into the child's being, is the habits he forms and the manner in which he expresses his relations to others. Just as the toilet training he receives in the nursing stage stays with him for life, so certain primary attitudes, confirmed by appropriate habits, tend to be incorporated in the personality. Here, in these earliest years, is the first critical stage in the child's development. The discipline of these years is a character-molding factor. The spirit in which discipline is conveyed, if it is conveyed at all, whether it is sympathetic and understanding or peremptory and harsh, all affect the extent to which the discipline is accepted and integrated or resented and in the course of time rejected.

Other critical situations may arise from the vicissitudes of schooling, where family direction and encouragement may prove decisive. These situations will be considered in the section which follows. Here we briefly refer to two other situations in respect to which the relation between parents and children becomes critical.

The first is the onset of puberty. On the whole, parents, at least in countries that have puritanic traditions, are peculiarly awkward in the way they instruct their children on this subject. Some evidence suggests that mothers are wiser with girls than fathers with boys. In any event, occasions occur that lead to bitter dissensions in the home, discussions which can start a train of troubles.

The other critical situations center round the choice of a career. Parents are frequently unable to understand that their children are not made in their own image. They want them to take up the parental interests and pursuits. Fathers on one social level want their sons to enter their own business or their own line of business; on another social level they are ambitious that their sons should rise in the world. Such desires are natural and proper enough, but when children insist on following their own road, when, for example, the son of a successful businessman is set on becoming an artist, a clash may occur that results in the youth's alienation from the family.

The types of parent-youth dissension we have mentioned become critical situations when family cohesion is loose, as is not infrequently the case. As the young are growing up, in the diversity of relationships and conflicting demands, the family scene is not unlikely to be a somewhat troubled one. This is the time when differences in early training and inculcated discipline bear their respective fruits.

It has long been recognized that family cohesion is much stronger in some groups than in others, and that juvenile delinquency is definitely less frequent where family cohesion is marked. It is not so well recognized that even in groups where family cohesion is weak, in the sense that the husband is none too faithful to his marriage vows but an authoritative value system is inculcated in the home, the delinquency rate is also likely to be low. The modes of training the young may differ, but all types emphasize respect by the young for their parents and elders, and the early indoctrination insists on some primary values that enshrine this attitude of respect. In a considerable majority of Jewish homes, for example, early training of this type, including the value of family cohesion, is the rule. In the traditional Chinese home, again, respect for family obligations is the very center of all ethical training. In the Mexican family, particularly in the less urbanized areas, the father is recognized as the source of authority, and whatever the relations between father and mother, respect for both and for elders in general is instilled into the children from the first. In other respects, the doctrinal upbringing in these three types of families is very dissimilar, but the common inculcation of a disciplined respect for parents is sufficient to insure a comparative absence of serious delinquency in the young. In families of these types, differences or clashes or rifts that in many American families would become trigger situations are overridden by the presence of fundamental loyalties.

From this point of view the traditional Mexican family, which is found with variations in other parts of Latin America, has a rather special interest. The roles of the father and mother are sharply differentiated. The male is the home authority, the female is the housekeeper. Both have their respective responsibilities. The mother is expected to be very "feminine" and self-effacing, but this by no means implies that she is weak or yielding in relation to the children. She can be quite authoritative in her appropriate field. The father may be somewhat careless about his marital relations, but because of the demarcation of roles that fact does not break up the family union, and even if the children become disillusioned about their father or actually afraid of him, his authority is still respected and their need for affection is satisfied through the much-enduring mother.[1]

One significant aspect of the Mexican situation is that broken families are considerably more frequent, at least among the lower class, than in the United States, as is shown by the 1950 census of Mexico, but under such conditions the traditional value system is maintained by the mother and respect for authority seems to endure in the children. Thus we find that in the traditional Mexican family neither the prevailing abject poverty nor the fact that the family is broken is conducive to much delinquency. The conclusion would appear to be that when the young are brought up from their earliest years within a clear-cut value system that sets a high premium on the authority of the elders the tendency to juvenile delinquency is low.

In sum, if one ventured to reduce to the simplest terms the

element of family training that is most essential as a safeguard against the development of delinquent attitudes, it would be the inculcation in the child of a *sense* of obligation. When this lesson is learned in the earliest years, clothed with the doctrinal authority of the elders, it is likely to endure and to remain a guide of life, no matter to what extent the young enter new areas of experience and follow new ways.

The School

Next in importance to what the family does for or to the young is what the school does for or to them. The school can be to the child a long stretch of drudgery and boredom, or a mixed experience of plodding work and joyful play, or a place where habits of learning are formed and new incentives aroused, or a not unpleasant refuge from the unhappiness of a wretched home. What happens through the years of growing up at school is always in the longer run crucial. How important it is for the future of the young is flagrantly illustrated by what happens when the school fails—though the failure is by no means always attributable to the school itself. The relation between drop-outs and delinquency is now a subject of great concern. The record is most revealing. "In 1952, 61 per cent of all delinquents between 8 and 17 years of age were not enrolled in school. . . . Ninety-five per cent of the 17 year olds adjudged delinquents were recorded as school drop-outs; 85 per cent of the 16 year olds. . . . Three out of five delinquents are school drop-outs."[2]

Other reports show that seriously retarded pupils have a much higher proportion of delinquency than pupils who make average or better grades.[3] The frequency of retardation is highly correlated with the slum conditions under which high delinquency rates prevail. School retardation is a link, effect and cause, in the vicious circle within which so many slum-bred children revolve. Education with adequate guidance, especially if well directed in the earliest school years, is a powerful agency to enable the youth to break out of the circle.

Critical schooling situations may occur at any stage from

the nursery school to the end of schooling. The initiation to school learning can itself be so unfavorable as to be traumatic. On the other hand, the very early redirection of offensive habits or of negligent attitudes can have an enduring effect that might be much harder to achieve at a later stage. The teacher can easily spot deficiencies that a parent, either through negligence or fondness, may fail to perceive or else to correct. Rifts with the parents may develop because the child is given a bad report, and the parents may take quite the wrong way of dealing with the situation. A school year with a dull or sarcastic or unsympathetic teacher may generate a lasting distaste for schooling, or the introduction to a new teacher who is stimulating and sympathetic may awaken an interest that grows stronger with the years. In fact, the most important lesson a training institute could offer to the prospective teacher would be to inculcate a realization that the first requisite of teaching is the ability to awaken interest and incentive in the pupil. Again, the bullying of a sensitive youth by a young ruffian may lead the former to play truant, with a train of consequences. Finally, for a brooding retarded pupil any school mishap or grievous home relationship or discouragement may be the breaking point at which the youngster becomes a drop-out. The school, as we show more fully in Part Three, has a great role to play in guiding the young, discovering the early signs that point to disturbance or maladjustment or disaffection and seeing that these receive the necessary attention and services, and thus above all preventing the development of tendencies that may mature into habitual delinquency.

The Peer Group

Delinquency, according to one viewpoint, is as much a matter of intimate association with a group engaged in this behavior as is the spirit of neighborly service engendered in a well-knit group of Boy Scouts. The delinquent tradition which continues to thrive in the slum neighborhoods of large urban centers, according to Cohen, offers a solution to the problems of the new entrants into a gang culture.[4] The choice for attachment to a

gang may have as many underlying reasons as there are indi-
viduals. A boy may choose his group for the sense of belonging
and security that he derives from being with those of similar
racial or ethnic background. Another may join a gang to avert
being attacked by its members. For some boys the attachment
to a delinquent gang helps to mitigate feelings of anxiety growing out of uncertainty about parental affection. Or a deep unconscious wish to be apprehended in order to expiate some fan-
cied guilt may lead them into a delinquent gang.[5]

Cohen points out that "the human personality is a complex
system with many roles, many activities, many aspirations and
many problems. The delinquent gang provides an outlet for
those who share a common core of problems." Since the delinquent gang is a joint enterprise where satisfaction is shared the
implication is that the sheer accessibility to other children who
have kindred problems may play an important part in the decision to join one. Once the delinquent subculture exists, it
may very well tip the scale in favor of participation by a boy as
a solution to his other problems as well.[6]

Another line of inquiry, as espoused by Ohlin and Lawrence,[7]
is concerned with interactions directed to changing the delinquent's mode of coherence to a deviant value system and thus
opening new opportunities that would lead away from violence.

As one means of early intervention in order to stall recruit-
ment of junior member gang groups by older gangs, the Henry
Street Settlement in New York established a predelinquent gang
project for boys aged eight to thirteen. The goal was to prevent
the "development of new gangs by weaning them away from the
older gangs."[8] The group work program was aimed at detaching
the young from gangs through the help of a skilled group
worker. Parents, too, met to consider the situations affecting
their children and learn how to provide greater regularity and
order in their lives. The director states that "when the adults
close ranks and stand together, the very ground these children
travel from home to various parts of the neighborhood became
more solid."[9]

In presenting a composite picture of youth for whom work

programs have meant an intervention in delinquent gang activity, the portrait of Charles emerges from the experiences of Mobilization for Youth. An eighteen-year-old drop-out, Charles left school in the tenth grade and had been a member of a bopping gang since he was thirteen, participating in the usual gang fights. His gang membership provided his only meaningful peer relationships. He was cynical, distrustful, and pessimistic about life. His pattern of coping with authority was "to play it cool." He had held three different jobs for an average of two months each, as a delivery boy, messenger, and factory floor boy, quickly losing interest in each job.[10]

At Mobilization for Youth he was enrolled in a building-maintenance work group which performed a variety of tasks for nonprofit agencies in the community. After seven months he was advanced to an on-the-job training program. The work groups of the program are structured to cut across ethnic, economic, and gang lines. The dominance of the goal of the work task itself provided motivation and opportunity for forming working relationships with strangers. In a number of the work groups, hostile gang groups were able to work out non-aggression pacts.

The work foreman was extremely important to Charles as a person requiring adherence to work regularity and as a male personality who was strong, fair, competent, and not to be "taken in." Charles began to see that "playing it straight" was neither so difficult nor so dangerous. Now that he worked, his mother's annoyance with his spending and his late rising hours was abated and she encouraged him in this new role. The work group introduced a new set of connections into his life. He found that his ties to some of his friends who were not working were weakened, since he had less time to be with them and their interests and concerns were no longer so similar to his. The older group thought he had "sold out," but having come under the influence of a new system of expectations, values, and behavior patterns, he felt a stronger bond with the work group. Since the work group is made up of neighborhood youth he is spared feelings of guilt and isolation.[11]

The Youth for Service program in San Francisco, developed
by the American Friends Service Committee, achieved notable
success in averting nearly all the gang rumbles it attempted to
stop. In two respects Youth for Service has achieved results
aspired to by many agencies. First, the program was successful
in attracting the boys it intended to reach. At one time the large
majority of participants were believed to have been "official delinquents" and members of San Francisco's toughest gangs.
Second, the agency's Inter-Club Council was successful in keeping the participation of many juvenile gang leaders and proved
an effective preventive against gang rumbles.[12]

A Central Harlem Street Club Project was conducted under
the auspices of the Committee on Street Clubs of the Welfare
Council of New York City. A series of gang wars was the impetus for the formation of the project. The street club workers
in the project worked with the gang boys to gain their acceptance and influence their group values. A major aim of the project
was to establish a procedure which would constrain the group
from participating in antisocial behavior provoked by their
"exaggerated need for status," their conception of the importance of being "tough," and their feeling of being in a "jungle."
Participation in constructive programs under the guidance of the
worker resulted in a lessening of such aggressive behavior as
gang fighting and stealing. Reefer smoking, drinking, and
gambling still went on. However, many boys did gain a new
confidence through learning to make their own decisions and
plans and to carry out responsibilities. Some of their negative
attitudes toward adults declined and they began to take a more
active and constructive interest in their neighborhoods.

The Over-all Increase
of Delinquency

Nearly all the serious research concerning the present delinquency situation has been directed to the relatively greater increase in some situations and under some conditions in comparison with others. There are obvious reasons why this should be so. In the first place, the high-delinquency areas, and generally the situations in which the volume of delinquency has risen sharply, attract more attention and call more immediately for preventive or remedial service. In the second place the techniques of the researcher are readily applicable to situations that yield specific correlations between the phenomenon under study and other variables, but when we are dealing with a phenomenon exhibiting itself under a great multiplicity of variant conditions over a very wide range, the problem of research is not only much more difficult but also one that is less susceptible of clearcut conclusions.

While scholars have shied away from the larger problem, popular opinion offers its diversified verdicts freely in the broadest terms. It attributes the general increase to the decay of morality, the falling away from religion, the materialism of the times, the corruption of political life, the freedom allowed modern youth and the general slackness of family discipline, the general habituation to violence accentuated by the exhibits of television, movies and comics, and the press, and finally to the insecurities and uncertainties generated by modern conditions and climaxed by the hazard of nuclear armaments in the hands of rival powers.

Obviously, we cannot directly trace the impact on youth of any or all of these conditions. The few more positive characteristics included in the list, particularly the influence of the movies and of television, have been the object of careful research, but very few definite conclusions have been reached. We cannot, however, dismiss these imputed causes on that account. The temper of the times must surely in some way register in the minds of the young.

Some modes of attribution sympathetically regarded by a number of scholars appear to us highly dubious. Society, a social historian once wrote, is the cause of crime—not some features of society but society as a whole. This is a truism that leads nowhere. In one meaningful sense, of course, society is the cause of crime, since there is no crime except where laws exist, and the code of laws is a social creation. It can also be said that the character of crime depends on the specific character of a society. You don't find a "black market" except where society through its government restricts the free sale of particular goods. People are not arrested for being out late at night unless there is a curfew, and nobody is put in prison for speaking against the government in a genuine democracy.

A somewhat more sophisticated form of the above-mentioned approach is the view that crime and delinquency are outcomes or by-products of the society's cultural values. In its usual form this doctrine assumes that delinquency is responsive to the examples or models set by parents and elders in general.[1] It may be the consequence of imitation, or of indoctrination, or of habituation to the mores prevalent in the society.

While no doubt the example of the elders has an important influence on the young, this whole mode of explanation is seriously defective. In the first place it offers no answer to our question concerning the general increase in delinquency. Aside from that, it gives a quite excessive role to imitation, the following of the model set by elders. Many youngsters react from the ways of the parents, and everywhere youthful peer groups associate and develop attitudes and form habits of their own. The difference between the generations is in a changeful society as noticeable as their resemblance. Moreover, for the areas of high delinquency—areas mostly of squalor and destitution— it would be extremely rash to conclude that the high rate is due to imitation. As we have already sought to show, the conditions of life in such areas breed tensions and frustrations with which the more susceptible youth are unable to cope, with the consequence that they tend to resort to delinquent ways. While down-and-outs, including the more ineffective type of criminal, gravitate to these areas, there is ample evidence that a large proportion of the residents where children get into trouble with the police are by no means the "models" these youngsters imitate. From personal experience the writer can testify that this conclusion held true for one high-delinquency neighborhood, largely inhabited by in-migrant Puerto Ricans, in which he organized a study.

The doctrine that the delinquency of the children reflects the delinquent attitudes of ther parents takes a number of forms. There is the straightforward hereditary theory of causation, the theory of the "bad seed." The classical illustration is the famous history of the Jukes and the Kallikaks, whose offspring over several generations were shown to be in so many instances criminals or ne'er-do-wells or feeble-minded.[2] There is the viewpoint that the "multiproblem" families are an enclave of their own, breeding their own kind. No one disputes the importance of heredity, but the more we learn about it the more we discover the variability of the stock. And we certainly must not discount the impact of environment. So long as the Jukes breed in a slum environment subject to the depressing influence and unwholesome example of their parents, we have no right to conclude that heredity alone is responsible for the behavior of the descendants. The trouble with all such theories is that they refuse to recognize the complex interplay of conditions from which social phenomena result.

At the other extreme from the hereditary doctrine there is the broad principle that parents one way or another are responsible for the sins of the children. The onus may be placed on the parents' failure to educate the children through disregard, neglect, or lack of proper discipline, or on unduly harsh discipline and excessive pressures on the children to meet the standards of achievement demanded by the parents. Again there can be no question that many parents are at fault in the upbringing of their children. Bernard Shaw had a point when he remarked that the only occupation for which no training is required is parenthood. But the influence of bad home training may be offset in a measure at least if the parents have the affection and respect of the children. And of course there are various other factors that determine the future of the child—school influences, peer-group influences, religious influences, timely guidance from a trusted counselor, and so forth. The record shows also that some children, including a number who later attained to fame, have reacted strongly against an evil or unhappy home environment, eschewing the ways of the parents.

None of the above-mentioned theories offers a logical explanation of our present problem, the over-all increase in the volume of delinquency not only throughout this country but across many other countries as well. The only way they could be directed to this end would be on the assumption that events or developments brought about by the older generation cause greater disturbances, tension, or disorientation in the younger generation than in the generation responsible. If, for example, delinquency is more prevalent in large cities and in industrialized areas, then the growth of industrialization would show an increase in delinquency in the next generation. The aftermath of war has also some association with the increase of crime and delinquency. We have not seen any attempt to follow up the general theory here indicated, but it is plausible and may well have some relevance.

Our own conclusions respecting the over-all increase of delinquency may be summed up as follows. From numerous studies we learn a great deal about the attitudes broadly characteristic of delinquent youth. We know the types of disturbances, the stresses and strains, that prompt a revulsion from indoctrinated ways; that provoke a rankling resentment, and often enough a rebelliousness against the established order as embodied in parents, teachers, and the official guardians of the law; that induce in some a certain restlessness, bravado, and aggressive push for status, and in others sullen withdrawal from participation in social ongoings or feelings of hopeless disorientation and lack of direction. A certain amount of delinquency is of course generated in other ways, through some conjunctures of conditions bearing on susceptible youth. Although for a relatively small number delinquency comes naturally, without inward strain, being nurtured by delinquent parents, it is most conspicuous where youth are subjected to thwarting circumstances that block and distort youthful aspirations. Such is the situation in our high-delinquency areas. And in areas where conditions are far less depressing, situations which put the young under severe strain can still occur. Delinquency might result, for example, from the impact on a sensitive child of family rifts and the domination of first one parent and then the other.

In general our evidence suggests that, so long as children are anchored in a system of relationships which provides the affection they need, commands their respect, and gives them room for expansion, they can for the most part take in stride the rank suggestions of some of the things they see and hear and read. The broad influences of the times are not likely to bite so deeply that young people will be jolted into delinquent ways on that account alone. The impact of changes in the daily life—increased mobility, social insecurities due to automation or other technological developments, any increase in the competitive struggle, any new conditions that tend to disturb old habituations or old beliefs—would certainly be of more direct importance. Such changes would be calculated to heighten tensions that are provoked by other circumstances. They could, in particular areas, make the differences that overcome the edgy resistance or weak equilibrium that some young people would otherwise maintain, causing some of those who not so long ago might have remained law-abiding to yield to additional stress. Such a changed situation might, moreover, be brought to bear indirectly through the influence of the changed conditions on parents and on the family life.

Since such new influences are not localized or confined to specific groups, their pervasive impact could explain the increase of delinquency beyond any national frontiers. It is widely believed, not without some grounds, that our civilization of today is peculiarly unsettled. The manner in which this unsettlement reaches into the world of the young, aggravating the difficulties of the transitions and readjustments that growing up imposes, might well be made the subject of broad-based inquiry.

Our conclusions here have had to be stated in this tentative fashion because the over-all problem has not received the scholarly attention it deserves. Every generation is reared in a different atmosphere from that of the preceding one. Even English "public school" boys, for all the pride of tradition, read different books, discuss different things, and respond differently to old usages in each succeeding generation. Sometimes the difference in atmosphere becomes especially marked because of far-reaching social changes or abrupt disturbances of the social order. Such changes have occurred in the lifetime of both the previous and the present generation. The convulsions of war and the transformations of ensuing peace have greatly affected every nation in the world. Everywhere youth faces new situations and new problems. It is no easy task to assess the influence of these changes on the minds of the young, but it should be by no means insuperable. Such an assessment would require comparative studies in various countries, on a cooperative basis. It would involve studies of the informal education of the young, of the various modes in which they adjust themselves to the life of the family, to the preparation for a career, and to the traditional standards of their elders. It would seek to probe their sense of values and their expectations and such differences as these might reveal between the outlooks of the younger and of the older generation, distinguishing the findings for various categories of the population. Comparative studies of the attitudes and rationalizations of delinquents of different classes and different countries could also throw some light on the issue.

Significant indications might also be derived from the recordings of a series of "bull sessions" so conducted that the youths attending them would feel free to express themselves with complete candor.

The many-nationed program sketched above would require extensive planning and rather substantial funds. But the reasonable chance that it would help to solve a problem so pressing and so important for the direction of the great amount of energy and resources devoted to this field would be eminently worthwhile. Without guidance of this sort we will be forced to remain in the twilight of conjecture.

9

Summation

Any social phenomenon so disturbing and so widespread as the more serious forms of juvenile delinquency is bound to arouse a great deal of speculation and a certain amount of research regarding its causes. Relatively little has been done, however, to clarify the problem. We have many conflicting theories, ranging from simple unchecked assumptions to the variant conclusions of practitioners and theorists representing different disciplines. The subject is still in a state of confusion.[1] In Part Two we have endeavored to analyze the issue, to point out the limitations of some current theories, and to present what we hope is a consistent interpretation of the problem.

An initial difficulty is the fact that the term "cause" is used in several different senses. It may refer to the particular conjuncture of conditions, to the situation that as a whole is different from other situations and thus evokes the differential phenomenon in question. Within this total situation there may be some factors that increase or diminish the range of the phenomenon. We dealt with this subject broadly in Part One, where we distinguished the conditions associated with high delinquency rates and sought to show that they were relevant, especially when we included the "psychic conditions" associated with delinquency in the lower-delinquency areas.

In the second sense of the term, "cause" refers to some particular factor that, when brought into relation to an appropriate set of conditions, evokes the phenomenon. We say, for example, that a carelessly flung match was the cause of a forest fire or that a spark was the cause of an explosion. So we have discussed the "trigger factor" or the "precipitant" that upsets an uneasy or unstable equilibrium and is decisive as a determinant of a course of action.

In the social sphere we can speak of cause in a third sense. We call negligence, for example, a cause—the failure to perform some act that would have prevented an accident or injury or loss. This is cause as responsibility. It may mean either performing an act or some program of action which we were obligated not to perform or failing to perform one which we were obligated to perform. In this broad sense we may say that some responsibility for delinquency rests on those officials or agencies that knowingly fail to take the available steps for its prevention or control. Likewise we say that a father is responsible for his son's delinquency if, being delinquent himself, he initiated his son into delinquent ways, or, again, if he is supine or careless in the training of his child. Responsibility, we observe, can be greater or less according to the circumstances.

Most problems of social causation concern not the presence or absence of a phenomenon, but the more or the less, the multiplicity or scarcity of the phenomenon, the manner and extent of its distribution. This fact introduces several complications into the search for the cause. It makes it less likely that we can find clean-cut wholly definite answers. Thus in the environment most prolific of cases of delinquency we find that a majority of young people are not delinquents; and, when we further take into account the type of mentality that in such an environment is prone toward delinquency, we still find others with similar mental attributes who are unaffected in this direction. Getting down to the precise causation of individual cases is therefore not feasible, and we must be content with the conclusion that under stipulated conditions a quite considerable incidence of delinquency is highly probable. This, however, is a sufficient guide to preventive measures and gives us a lead for the application of remedial services. This is the subject that will occupy us in Part Three.

When we are concerned with the greater or smaller incidence of delinquency over a very wide area, when, as at present, we are faced with a general increase in its incidence over at least a great portion of the civilized world, then the problem of causation becomes much harder to investigate. The "less" in this situation is the tendency to delinquency in a previous period over this wide range, the "more" is the incidence over that range today. Comparisons of conditions then and now are obscured by the multitude of variant changes over so vast a terrain. The only lead comes from the knowledge, based on more specific comparisons and some general considerations, that an increase in tensions and pressures and a weakening of convictions and of the sense of security are conditions that tend to weaken the spirit of law-abidingness and the belief in authority and thus to promote delinquency.

Part Three

STRATEGIC

APPLICATIONS

10

Broad Considerations on Strategy

In Part One we reviewed the various social, environmental, and psychological conditions that characterize areas with higher and lower incidences of youthful delinquency. We noted in particular that distinctively high rates of delinquency are generally found in close correspondence with high rates of other sociopathological phenomena, such as economic dependence, infant mortality, admissions to mental hospitals, psychiatric clinic cases, insanitary housing; all these in turn being associated with slum conditions in our great cities. In other words, very high delinquency was itself a symptom of a serious total maladjustment of a population to the mode of existence in which it found itself, a situation determined in the first instance by squalid poverty and usually aggravated by social discrimination. The superficial judgment that the people themselves, the families living under these conditions, are to blame is irrelevant, even if it were well founded. We don't refuse to treat people for their diseases because these have resulted from their own neglect or carelessness or folly. Effective remedial treatment is important for the welfare of the community as a whole as well as for the victims of disease. *We can conclude that so long as such breeding grounds of delinquency remain, relatively high delinquency will endure.*

Important as this consideration is, it deals with only one aspect of a many-sided problem. Even in the areas of worst delinquency there are large numbers of young people who do not become delinquents under the pressures and deprivations of their social and physical environment. We saw, moreover, that the probability that a youth growing up within that environment will become delinquent depends not only on the character of the specific family life he shares but also on the specific mental make-up of the youth himself. Everywhere there are significant variations in conditions and in the response of youth to them. The same statement holds of course for youth in lower-delinquency areas. Delinquency is a mode of response to pressures and to incitations that develop in every area of society. Susceptibility to delinquency is highly variant both in degree and in type.

In Part Two we sought to draw some conclusions respecting the causation of delinquency. We regarded the fact that high-delinquency areas are high-rated also for a whole series of socio-pathological conditions characterizing urban slums as bearing out the conclusion that the delinquency in question is not to be attributed to a natural tendency inherent in the ethnic groups involved, but rather to the strains, handicaps, and family troubles to which their young people are exposed. Obviously this points to a different mode of treatment than would be applicable if we regarded it as due primarily to the cause as moral obliquity or the "bad seed." To understand the incidence of delinquency as it varies in different situations we must get down to the conjuncture of predisposing conditions that affects the respective reactions of youth of diverse mentalities. While it has long been recognized that certain conditions—the inadequacy of family relations and of family disciplines, the pull of youthful associations, the frustrations that balk ambitions and aspirations, and so forth—are conducive to delinquency, we must recognize also that the degree to which young persons resist or respond to them, the alleviations and the acerbations of these influences, the character of the breaking point that changes predisposition to commitment, are endlessly variant.

In keeping with these findings, we analyzed and criticized the various theories that offer a bloc explanation of high-level delinquency by attributing it to the "culture" of a lower social class or to the impact of middle-class standards on lower-class mores. For the same reasons we reject any theory that lays predominant stress on any one of a series of interdependent factors, whether on heredity, somatic structure, very early conditioning, or social environment. In every situation there are conditions which predispose and also conditions that in varying degrees counteract or negate the predisposing conditions. Under the worst environmental conditions a large proportion of the young do not become habitual delinquents. Recently there has been increasing evidence of the amount of delinquency in well-established families; perhaps here too we would find that below the surface of respectable well-being discord and maladjustment not infrequently lurk, or parental evasion of and disrespect for law sets a bad example.

While we cannot in our theory of causation assign predominance to any one of a number of interdependent factors, for purposes of strategy we must lay particular stress on the conditions that are more amenable to control. If the conditions are really interdependent, our ability to deal with any of them may suffice to arrest or counteract the resort to delinquency. Obviously, the physical environment (say the city slum) and certain unfavorable features of the social environment, such as the lack of opportunity, training, guidance, or protection, can be changed, controlled, or compensated for.

The considerations advanced in Parts One and Two lead us to certain more specific conclusions with respect to strategy. Actually many of these conclusions can be derived from common sense and from experience, but they are reinforced by the researches discussed in Part One and by the reflections on causation adduced in Part Two.

1. The prevention of delinquency is more feasible, less costly, and more promising than later efforts toward rehabilitation.

Every effort should be made to improve our programs of rehabilitation, but fewer would need them if we had more regard for prevention. There is practically universal agreement that the earlier we can bring guidance, protection, care, and therapy to those who show signs of needing this help, the better will be the results. Yet, although there has been some real progress in the last few years, we still expend the greater part of our available resources on rehabilitation programs that unhappily have had only rather disappointing results. Moreover, much of the preventive work is inadequately directed and is not followed through.

We need in the first place to broaden some prevailing conceptions of what a genuine program of prevention involves. The provision of opportunities for ball games and dance parties and club quarters and so forth is certainly desirable and salutary, but it reaches only to the outskirts of preventive work. The problems of troubled or difficult youth are too complex and deep-seated to be solved that way. We may broadly distinguish three types of service that have greater significance.

First, there are the broad-based educational services that do not limit instruction merely to a routine curriculum in the three "r's" but are calculated to spur incentive, to awaken the mind to a rich world of opportunity, to reveal the values of the good life, and to upbuild morale to face life's problems. Such education is not to be thought of as merely preventive, as a safeguard against getting into trouble, but as the positive preparation all youth need. Nor is it a service by any means exclusive to the school; the home, the church, agencies of various kinds have important roles to play in it, but they can do it only as far as they understand the problems of the young and the approaches without which no teaching is effective. In this area the more particular function of the school is to stimulate the live interest of the pupil in the process of learning by reaching out to whatever capacities or aptitudes he may possess. Unhappily, in much of our schooling this role is very imperfectly fulfilled, and the consequences are more serious than we generally recognize.

Furthermore, the majority of school children do not proceed to college, and therefore it is incumbent on the school to prepare its pupils not only for the business of being citizens but also for their working life, training them in the basic requirements of accuracy, clear observation of details, concentration of attention, the fundamental qualities necessary for any kind of effective operation. In our present-day society many teen-agers on leaving school face the threat—and the fact—of unemployment, without prospect of a career. Nothing could be more demoralizing, and the community, in cooperation with the school, can and should take whatever steps are necessary to ensure that employment, really useful employment, is found or made for them and that they are trained to take it. Besides its other advantages such a policy becomes a very important means for the prevention of delinquency.

One of the most hopeful developments at the present time is the increasing recognition that the young in poverty-stricken areas must be trained in the kind of skills that are potentially within their range and are adapted to changes in the labor market. The fact that the percentage of unemployment among these youths is about twice as large as that among young people in general is sufficiently indicative of the educational and social handicaps from which they suffer. The training must be thorough and realistic. With the advance of automation hard manual tasks are at a discount but opportunties in a variety of service jobs and those using minor mechanical skills are likely to increase. The school should be geared to provide more of this preparatory training than it usually does, in addition to the specially established community provision under the new poverty-area programs.

Anything that increases the range of opportunity, especially for the poor and disprivileged, or helps develop in the young a sense of belonging, of effective membership within the community (and in this connection the reduction of ethnic or racial discrimination is of prime importance), serves as a safeguard against youthful delinquency.

The second type of significant service is concerned with preventive measures specifically directed to those young persons who are in immediate need of guidance and protection. These are requisite for all youth in high-delinquency areas and for near-delinquents and incipient delinquents wherever they can be found. This type of direct service has been curiously slow to be undertaken and developed, even though both common sense and the testimony of authorities emphasize the advantages of early treatment, before habit and associations confirm the tendency to delinquency and before the teen-ager has come to regard authority with enmity. Few thoroughgoing projects of this kind have been undertaken. The writer, as director of the City of New York's Juvenile Delinquency Evaluation Project, was enabled with the assistance of the President of the City Council and the Mayor, to establish one in a high-delinquency neighborhood of the South Bronx. We were able to find a number of young persons who were beginning to get into trouble and who otherwise might well have escaped notice. Some boys came and asked us to provide a leader for their group, since otherwise they might have been drawn into some trouble-making gang. Our contacts with neighborhood volunteers, with neighborhood churches and schools, revealed how ample was the opportunity and how great the need. Unfortunately, the program ceased to exist in the form in which we had envisioned it when we finished our commission from the City, too soon for its methods to be tested and its results evaluated.

Two major foci from which this type of early prevention program can be conducted are the neighborhood and the school. The lines of a neighborhood program—the neighborhood being here understood to be the narrowest urban area that can be readily distinguished as possessing or potentially possessing some demographic characteristics of its own—are clearly established. Such a program needs in the first place a small professional staff to be located in the neighborhood: a director, one or two child-welfare specialists and community organizers, and a research worker. These will enlist neighborhood volunteers and a neighborhood committee to help in a secondary program for the discovery of vulnerable youngsters and to provide first aid and arrange for follow-ups, to make referrals where therapy is needed and see that the referrals are carried through, and so forth.

2. The rescue of delinquent or near-delinquent youth cannot be effectively undertaken unless those who are assigned to

this service are properly qualified by training and experience, possessing also the attributes of character that enable them to understand the diverse problems of troubled or disturbed youngsters.

With some notable exceptions, the tendency still prevails in the official service to assume that anyone with a firm hand and a modicum of training can cope with the emotional and social problems of the young. It is assumed that while the higher-ups, the real professionals need special training and competence, the people who work "at the face," so to speak, who are in most direct touch with youthful offenders, can get along all right with less. The policeman, in whose discretion it lies, within limits, to warn the youth or to see that a report is made out for parent or guardian or to make an arrest, often has quite inadequate training for the job. Not infrequently he adopts rough and ready methods, sometimes with needless harshness. The arrested youth may be placed in detention prior to court appearance and may find detention an unhappy and stigmatic experience. Then he comes before a judge. The adjudication that follows may be decisive for his future. The judge, who has the discretion to dismiss or discharge the case, to place the youngster on probation, or to commit him to an institution, is a political appointee. He may have little comprehension of the problems of the young and generally has an overcrowded calendar, which may cause him to make a rather hasty decision.

If the juvenile offender is placed on probation, he is presumptively under the charge of a probation officer. Probation means that the offender is being given an opportunity to make good. He needs guidance, counsel, protection, new associations. But very frequently the function of the probation officer is no more than to see that he keeps out of trouble, which means only that no new law violation is recorded against him. Of all the major services rendered to delinquents this one is often enough the most perfunctory and unsatisfactory, and in many areas the probation officer lacks the standing and the training his task demands.

If the offender is committed to an institution, he enters a

situation in which he mixes with other offenders and since they
are all chafing at the restraints of confinement a spirit of rebellion is rife and tends to frustrate the best efforts of the staff. The
institution finds it difficult to secure adequate "cottage parents"
(with whom the inmate spends much of his time), or guards
who sympathize with the policies of the institution, or even
counselors who are sufficiently qualified and willing to work
under these difficult conditions.

What we have said in the preceding paragraphs is a broad
assessment of a general situation, based on considerable evidence and on the writer's own experience. But there are notable
exceptions—services, programs, and institutions that are admi-
rably meeting the many problems they encounter, and some
others that are making progress in that direction. There are
police departments that maintain a well-equipped and well-
trained youth division. There are some highly qualified and devoted judges. There are a few probation systems that achieve
high standards, and others that strive to do so in spite of inadequate resources. There are a number of custodial institutions
for juveniles that are admirable of their kind, doing all they can
to fulfill a difficult and often baffling service. On every level we
find some workers who are dedicated and competent. But the
over-all improvement of our programs for delinquents will remain halting and sluggish until there is a much wider practical
recognition that the everyday tasks of those who work with or
for disturbed and troubled youngsters require high qualities of
mind and heart and that therefore *the status, standards, and
salaries of these workers must be raised.* At the time of writing
a new illustration of the failure to recognize those facts has come
to our attention. The New York State Judicial Conference has
organized a review of the conditions and ratings of the probation
services within the City. It has been the practice to put the
qualifications and salaries of the probation officers of the superior courts well above those of the courts that deal with juveniles
and adolescents. A group that should know better has appealed
to the Conference to maintain the differential, the assumption
being that probation work with juveniles is less demanding and

less important than that with adult offenders. Nothing could be further from the fact.

3. Officials appointed to organize or administer antidelinquency programs, whether under public or private auspices, should themselves be familiar with the problems of youth and should be in a position to keep in touch with developments in treatment and with the results of research.

4. The over-all planning of a city's programs and policies concerned with the control of delinquency, and more broadly with youth problems, should be administered by a special supervisory and planning unit of high competence, located within the city government in a position where its recommendations will carry most weight—preferably within the office of the Mayor.

The reasons back of our last two conclusions are obvious enough. The fuller significance and the practical application of the four conclusions we have stated will be presented in the remainder of this work.

11

The School

The great majority of children spend approximately twelve formative years in school, presumably under the watchful eyes of trained educators. The school cannot educate these children unless it makes them receptive to education, unless it awakens incentive and aspiration in them, unless it guides them over the distractions, disturbances, and inertias that block the educational process. While this statement holds for schools of every kind, it has a special significance for schools that serve the disprivileged, the children of groups subject to discrimination and prejudice, those who come from uncultured homes, those whose native language is other than the English, in short, those who are in any way educationally disadvantaged. Today in the United States one out of every three children comes from a low-income family.[1] The percentage has been increasing and present forecasts indicate that it may rise still higher.

There is ample evidence that these children need special training and guidance. There is convincing evidence that they are not receiving it in any adequate way. Tests given in grade schools or specific areas show an almost normal distribution of intelligence for such children in the first and second years, with a regular decrease in mean scores year by year until in the ninth grade the once "normal" group had become the "retarded" group.[2] The same type of regression is shown on test scores in reading and other subject-areas. Relatively few children of these "minority" groups complete academic high school courses and fewer still ever enter college.

The bearing of these factors on the future well-being of the child and in particular on his proneness to delinquency is surely obvious. It has been estimated that about 20 per cent of the school population suffers from emotional disturbances sufficiently marked to require intensive personal or small-group guidance and that about 10 per cent is in need of clinical treatment.[3] Some evidence of the schism between the child and the school is revealed in the fact that in 1952, 62 per cent of all delinquents between eight and seventeen were not enrolled in school. Truancy is not necessarily a precursor of delinquency, yet almost every delinquent has truanting on his record and 25 per cent of all delinquents have been identified as chronic truants. Retardation, with all it implies in the blighting of prospects and in its association with truancy, contributes also to delinquency proneness—and we have very good reason to believe that retardation itself is by no means solely or even mainly due to innate incapacity for learning.[4]

Our first conclusion, then, is that the educational guidance problem of difficult and troubled children has been sadly underestimated in most school systems of our large cities, where the need for such guidance is greatest. But a new awareness of the need is already spreading across the land and new programs and experiments to meet it are springing up. A poll of 1400 elementary and secondary school principals showed a growing emergence of these new patterns.[5] We shall briefly indicate the various lines along which these new programs are proceeding.

First, there are programs designed as a breakaway from the old system of moving omnibus classes from grade to grade, without regard for individual capacities and often without consideration of the readiness of some pupils for entrance to a higher grade. One plan is to organize tracks (fast, average, slow, remedial) for the grouping of pupils within grades, on the theory, which is still subject to examination, that pupils do better when they compete with pupils of relatively equal ability. Another, revolting against the elementary school tradition of having every subject taught for most of the day by a single teacher in the same room, has the children move from room to room to be taught various subjects by more specialized teachers. A third plan gives a team of teachers joint responsibility for the instruction among them of, say, 200 pupils. A more revolutionary system uses ungraded schools in which youngsters advance in one or another subject according to their ability. This approach, first tried out in Milwaukee some twenty years ago, presumably gives both the slower learners and the quicker the opportunity to learn at their own speed without undue criticism and without the sense of frustration.[6] The Norwalk School Improvement Program provides transitional classes for children who are backward because of socioemotional difficulties, and a considerable variety of programs offering special counseling, remedial reading, guidance for potential drop-outs, and compensatory aid for educationally disadvantaged children.[7]

Many schools adopt the principle of dividing the pupils in any grade into sections according to IQ or performance record. Usually the low IQs and the slow learners are placed in smaller sections, each numbering perhaps 15 or 20 pupils—a very proper consideration. There are obvious advantages in the procedure, but also some disadvantages. The latter can be partly met where special care is taken to transfer children from lower to higher categories when they show signs of improvement. But further exploration of the method is called for. In some systems "special service" schools are used for highly disadvantaged pupils or more generally for those who live in slumlike areas where initially the children have, for the most part, cultural, economic, and social handicaps.

The combination of teaching, guidance, and discriminating attention to individual needs might very well, as experience has already shown, be provided not only for obviously disadvantaged pupils but for all. It was this consideration that led the New York City Board of Education to inaugurate its well-known Higher Horizons program.[8] A demonstration guidance project in a racially integrated high school has shown how minority-group children of previously mediocre achievement could, given special attention, reach higher academic standards. The results as recorded were very convincing, some of these children rising to the top of very large classes. Higher Horizons, organized at the junior high school level for all the children in the selected grades and now including grades 3 to 5 in the elementary school, provides special class guidance and small-group counseling, "inspirational" talks from business leaders and professional people, trips to places of interest, information about occupations and prevocational instruction, conferences with parents, and efforts to enlarge the cultural experience of the pupils. An interesting feature of the experiment is the number of contacts the pupils make with others besides the school teachers, including volunteers, assistant college students, as well as various types of professionals. This is a wide-flung system of operations, and there are some grounds for believing the content is spread too thin, as the endeavor has been made to include more and more schools within the program. But the value of the principle has been established beyond question.

Another program under the auspices of the New York City Board of Education, one of particular significance, is the All-Day Neighborhood Schools.[9] These schools are situated in the most depressed and deteriorated areas of the city. In addition to the regular teaching staff a group of specially qualified teachers, usually six for each elementary school, and generally a community coordinator as well, is in attendance from 11 A.M. to 5 P.M. During school hours the members take charge of groups of pupils who need special coaching or guidance. From 3 to 5 P.M. they direct "clubs" of pupils, one for each grade, for supervised play, the clubs being composed of children selected because on one ground or another they particularly need to be looked after. During the play period a psychologist as well as the teacher keeps a watchful eye for signs of emotional disturbance or other behavior difficulties. In the evenings the schools are open for meetings with parents or for discussions with neighborhood officers. In various ways the schools thus live up to their name as all-day centers for neighborhood service. In addition they endeavor to make good the cultural deficiencies of the youngsters, practically all of whom come from deprived homes. The special merits of these schools, which are somewhat more expensive to operate, have not received the amount of recognition and support accorded to the Higher Horizons program.

Finally, under the New York City school system, after-school study centers have recently been established in some 230 schools situated in impoverished areas, mostly in elementary schools but including also some academic and vocational high schools. The objective is to provide disadvantaged youngsters a further opportunity to remove, through group and tutorial instruction, their educational lags.

The Role and Status of the Teacher

We have been specifying some of the distinctive programs that are being directed to the clamant need for more, and more effective, guidance and remedial service in the educational process. But for educational efficacy something else is clearly needed. The service a teacher can render depends on the qualifications of the teacher himself—even more, we venture to say, than on the programs he is called on to administer. It is also, in some measure, dependent on the freedom of the teacher to devote his time as fully as possible to the prime business of teaching.

Let us consider the second point first. The teacher is burdened with a variety of professional and nonprofessional duties. With large classes he has problems of gaining attention, maintaining discipline, and looking into special cases, absences, and the details of a variety of children's problems. He—more frequently she—has a plethora of forms to fill out, records to keep, exercises to check over, materials to prepare, as well as school-housekeeping chores. Together these occupy a considerable portion of the teacher's working time. There is too little left to attend to or even observe the learning difficulties of individual children. The result is mass education.

One experiment to alleviate this situation has been the enlistment of trained teacher aides, as tried out, for example, in the Bay City schools under the lead of Central Michigan College.[10] Preliminary reports showed a higher achievement level for the classes in which the plan was tried out. There is, however, some controversy over the merits of the plan, and at best it can be only a palliative. In-service training courses and workshops for instruction in guidance procedures in dealing with troubled or refractory children are very important and should be expanded and developed, since the average teacher is by no means competent to deal with the very difficult problems they pose.

The overcrowding of the schools and the shortage of teachers demand far more thoroughgoing remedies. There is an active shortage of teachers, to the extent that substitutes for regularly certified teachers often have to be employed, but more fundamental is the matter of the status and standards of the teaching profession as a whole. There are some excellent and devoted teachers and there are some really fine schools with strong leadership. But it is abundantly clear that, in spite of recent improvements and the valiant efforts some school boards are making, the status of the profession is too low and the salary rates do not compare with those of other professions. School teaching is the least regarded of the greater professions, and its practitioners have the least control over their conditions of work. We need more and better schools and we need more and better teachers, but this primary need, on which the welfare of our youth so largely depends, cannot be satisfied until the value of the teaching service is more fully realized by the community as a whole. Something can be accomplished by far-reaching changes in the training demanded for the profession, and on this point we are in agreement with the admirable study by Dr. James Conant.[11] Since it is not, however, within the province of this report to develop the subject, we shall be ʌtent to point out why this matter is so important for the prevention of juvenile delinquency.

Delinquency and the Educational Process

We saw in Part One that high delinquency rates are strongly correlated with sociopathological factors and inferior health conditions, a complex that is characteristic of slum poverty. We must also remember that high delinquency is correlated with low school ratings, considerable reading retardation, truancy, and leaving school early largely by dropping out. Add to this the consideration that it is the disadvantaged and discriminated-against ethnic and racial groups who are mostly the victims of this total complex of evils.

The educational aspects of this complex are the ones that concern us here. The complex itself will endure as long as the slum environment and the conditions that create it continue to exist, but much can be done in the meantime to improve the life chances of the young people of these areas, especially if remedial steps and new opportunities are provided for them at an early enough age. Here is where the role of the school is of signal importance.

The conclusions of many researchers converge to show how greatly the life chances of children are affected by their educational deficiencies. They also show that in many cases these deficiencies are associated with emotional or mental disturbances as well as with the handicaps of poor earlier schooling and with the cultural poverty of the children's families. *These facts make it abundantly clear that to give such children a proper educational opportunity the schools must provide thorough-going guidance programs and incentive programs.*

The evidence for the relation of educational backwardness with delinquency is ample. In our Juvenile Delinquency Evaluation Project we found that the pupils in the special schools for disturbed or refractory children ("600" schools) were retarded in reading some 4 or 4½ years.[12] When one considers that average reading standards in our schools are themselves often far from adequate, this means that these children are practically illiterate. The same conclusion holds for the majority of juveniles who are committed to institutions. In the Quincy, Mass. public school it was found that 17 per cent of the pupils in special classes for very low IQ children and 31 per cent of the group designated as "slow learners" were known to the court.[13] Fabian recorded that 83 per cent of a sample of delinquent and pre-delinquent children had reading disabilities.[14] Roman reported that 84 per cent of the cases carried by the treatment clinic of Manhattan's children's court were severely retarded in reading. Many more studies could be cited as revealing the same correlation.[15]

The statistics on drop-outs offer further confirmation. As of the end of June 1955, of all inmates under the age of 25 who were under sentence in Federal courts only 6 per cent had completed high school.[16] The delinquency rate among Seattle drop-outs was reported as being twelve times that of those who stayed on in school, while in Bridgeport it was eight times as great.[17] Various other evidences point in the same direction. It is clearly indicated also (1) that a much higher percentage of drop-outs belonged to immigrant minority groups, Southern Negroes in Northern cities and Puerto Ricans; (2) that a larger proportion of these youth fail to find employment in their upper teens; and (3) that unemployed drop-outs figure most frequently in our delinquency statistics.

We have already noted that emotional disturbances are frequently associated with delinquency. Such disturbances may well arise from or at least be accentuated by failure at school. Retardation is apt to evoke feelings of inadequacy and frustration. To drop out is itself a confession of failure. Truancy cuts off the pupil from the prospect of a career, leads to bad associations, and creates fear and dislike of constituted authority. Many backward children develop a sense of alienation from schooling that is a prelude to further troubles. It is entirely likely that these unsatisfactory school relationships contribute to insecurity and its attendant evils. To whatever aspect of the whole complex of the causation of delinquency we turn we find the same vicious circle in operation. The school, though sometimes contributory to it, can also be a potent means of breaking it.

Some Special-Objective Programs

Much of the service the school can render in the prevention of delinquency is at the same time beneficial to all school children. This applies, for example, to guidance programs, whether specifically for educational guidance or for behavioral or vocational guidance, and also in considerable measure to reading instruction. Special remedial reading courses are necessary for those whose reading ability is abnormally low. It is our conviction, based on considerable experience, that reading standards are generally far too low, and *that much more attention should be given in teacher training and in curricular adaptations to raise the over-all level of this most essential instruction.*

Among more specialized programs we place first and foremost that of *early identification of problem children.* Programs of this type are still far too few. It is the most obvious of principles, but in this field one is tempted to say the least regarded, that the earlier any trouble is located and diagnosed the greater the chance that treatment will effect a cure. Most commonly recognized is the "acting out" youngster who is noisy and fractious. But there may be serious maladjustment gnawing at children who are recessive and introvert or at most sulky. It requires patience and skill to discover the problems of children, and teachers no less than guidance counselors should be taught the symptoms. Discovery is, of course, only the beginning; it must be followed by early care. The principal of a New York City school once told the writer about one or two students who in later years were involved in felonies. She said she reported the matter early in the elementary school history of the cases, but the only action taken was a filed report, with no follow-up, indicating minor adjustment difficulties. This, we should add, happened a decade ago, and important developments have taken place in this school system since then. The kindergarten and first years of elementary schooling represent the stage at which identification of trouble should begin, as has been pointed out, for example, in a study under the Santa Barbara school system, and as leading authorities, such as Dr. Marion Kenworthy, have insisted.

New York City a few years ago inaugurated an early identification program for kindergarten and the first three grades, with emphasis on the second grade. It is significant that first-grade teachers indicated that from 85 to 90 per cent of the children given attention had both learning problems and social or emotional problems, reading difficulties being most apparent.[18] Another program for the elementary school, the junior guidance program, provides special classes through grades 2 to 6 for disturbed children who fail to respond to classroom teaching. Attached to the program are full-time counselors and therapists. Specially trained teachers are also provided. The counselors focus on the relation of parents to children, since so often the disturbance of the child has its root in the home situation.[19] In still another program therapeutic play groups (led by specially trained guidance counselors) are set up and function as a guidance service to a limited number of elementary schools.[20]

New York City has developed also a special type of school for children with whom the regular school claims to be unable to cope. The objective was to place these children under special teachers, to surround them with special guardianship, and to provide a training program adapted to their behavioral and educational troubles, in the hope that a number of them could be restored to the regular schools. In the early stages the experiment was not successful, except as a means of "containing" incorrigibles. None went back to the regular schools, and relatively little progress of any kind was registered. Screening for admission was by no means satisfactory. More recently, under a change of management and enough critical recognition of the deficiencies of the system, some distinct progress has been made. A new assessment of them is now being planned.

The antipoverty program under the auspices of the Office of Economic Opportunity holds good promise of new developments in the raising of the educational level of disprivileged children, since nothing can do more to abolish poverty than the removal of educational deficiency combined with equal opportunity to utilize educational advancement. One promising new program of this kind is Operation Headstart, as initiated under the New York City Board of Education. In the summer of 1965 this program was inaugurated for preschool children suffering from disabilities and educational lags. The first effort met with various difficulties, on the one hand delays in making appropriations and on the other inadequate methods of discovering the appropriate children and developing the program. Nevertheless, the reception of it was very encouraging and no less than 23,000 children received a beneficial initiation. Experience has been gained and the effort is to be continued. One definite good was that it brought backward or untrained parents into new, helpful relations with the schools, to which for the first time they had ready access. Similar service can be and is being rendered by some day-care programs, which might very well be brought into close relation with Headstart and indeed with the whole range of community services for the very young.

Some school systems do not regard special classes as an answer to the problem of difficult children. Thus the Union Free School District No. 16 at Elmont, Long Island,[21] depends rather on special teachers and on providing extra periods of art, music, physical education, and so forth, adapted to the particular needs of individual pupils. Exceptional children are grouped for programs housed outside the school, at some convenient location within the community. For the individual coaching and guidance involved, the regular teaching staff was not sufficient, and a number of mothers in the community were selected as volunteer aides, working in close contact with the school district psychologist, physician, and psychiatric consultant. The assumption is that selected but not special trained persons, when duly oriented and supervised, can be of effective help in meeting the need some children have for one-to-one relationships within the teaching process. The degree of success that attends this effort will deserve careful study.

We turn next to *programs to rescue drop-outs*. We use

the word "rescue" advisedly. To take a drop-out back to school, under the power of the law, may be worse than futile, it may be harmful. The writer recalls an occasion when he met a judge of a children's court just after he had finished his day on the bench. He looked melancholy and on being asked what troubled him replied, "I have just sent a lad back to school and I know it was a bad thing to do." The youth in question was fifteen years of age, had come to dislike school and was troublesome there. He had dropped out, falsified his age to get a job, and was driving a truck, giving most of his earnings to support his mother and generally behaving well. It was useless to force schooling on an unwilling youth at that age, where he merely wastes his time in resentful restraint. The majority of drop-outs in the city in which this case occurred belong to in-migrant groups, Negroes, Puerto Ricans, and Mexicans, who for various reasons find it difficult to feel at home in public schools, a fact which incidentally raises another problem besides that of drop-outs as such.

Actually the drop-out rate has been decreasing over a number of years, but we can take little comfort from that fact. Not only does it remain true that considerably more than a fourth of the children entering school never graduate from high school, while a probable tenth do not finish the eighth grade, but also the chances for employment for ill-educated and semi-illiterate teen-agers are much more bleak than they used to be. With the mechanical advancement of our industrial system the demand for unskilled labor is greatly restricted and whole categories of unskilled jobs are being done away with. This fact has special significance for the in-migrants—Southern Negroes, Puerto Ricans, Southern Appalachian whites, Latin Americans—who come to urban areas with the cultural and socioeconomic conditioning of rural life.[22] Schooling should be, but frequently is not, adapted to preparing them for different conditions of living and of employment.

The two primary factors in the situation are the holding power of the schools—in other words, their ability to retain the pupil population in school until graduation—and the preventive means that can be employed to retain greater numbers. It would

appear from an intensive federal project instituted in 1962 that
in the thirty years preceding this investigation the holding power
of schools generally has increased for pupils from the fifth grade
through to graduation.[23] Gratifying as this is, it also throws a
dismal light on the previous situation, since the number of drop-
outs is still a serious problem. This drop-out rate is highest in
large cities and rural districts. In cooperation with eighty-nine
secondary schools in New York State the New York City Bureau
of Guidance conducted a holding-power project between 1952
and 1960. While its identification of probable drop-outs was
reasonably accurate, its proposals for reducing the drop-out rate
did not go very far. The schools with lower drop-out rates were
also more successful in efforts for further improvement.[24] However, the schools with fewer drop-outs were situated in the
better residential areas, and this obvious fact simply accentuates
another obvious fact—that the family situation is itself a potent
determinant of the drop-out problem. We have some evidence
that the responsibility rests not so much with family pressure on
the youth to add some earnings to the family budget as with
the lack of standards and the low level of aspiration characterizing so many families that have become inured to living in the
squalor of the slum. The family attitude conspires with the retardation and consequent alienation from school that for reasons
already mentioned the youth of these families are not unlikely
to experience, and the drop-out is the consequence. Some
studies speak of new "techniques" to retain children in school,
but the pedagogical resort to techniques is out of focus here. On
the one side, the teacher must endeavor to understand the problems of vulnerable youth and adapt this teaching to what they
can take, seeking always to stir their incentive to learn. On the
other side, the family must be aided, encouraged, and instructed
so that it cooperates with the school in its endeavor to educate
the pupil. Neither task is an easy one.

We have touched here on the third of the special problems of
the school, *that of the preparation of the pupils for their working life.* If the school is to educate the child to become an effective member of society or, if you prefer, to develop his poten-

tialities as a human being, it must prepare him for the workaday world, the changeful world of our times. In doing so it must take realistic cognizance of the aptitudes, conditions, and needs of different pupils. The task will differ somewhat for school populations of different areas. But there is a common core of instruction that all students need, no matter what their abilities or their backgrounds. This is not so much a question of subject matter as of approach. Every pupil needs to be taught to be observant, to make clear distinctions, to report accurately, to notice the way things are patterned. Such training is useful for all jobs, from the lowest to the highest, and with such training a young person can advance to the extent of his ability. Every pupil has some aptitude, some latent interest that intelligent instruction can evoke. Some respond readily, with others patient work is necessary to arouse interest. This consideration should be the basis of the vocational guidance that a large number of pupils need.

Some efforts are being made in this direction. The career guidance project in the New York City schools arose out of concern in the junior high school division for potential drop-outs, pupils whose adjustment to schooling was very poor and who also often had emotional and behavioral difficulties.[25] The project embraces thirty junior high schools distributed over four boroughs and concentrates on restoring the confidence and incentive of children who have experienced a long series of failures and frustrations. Already the program is claimed to have paid off in better attendance, improved attitudes and behavior, better study habits, and more desire to learn. An older out-of-school youth guidance center program for senior teenagers in New York City has in the past two years been making special efforts to reach drop-outs; it provides opportunities for vocational training and personal guidance.[26] It reports some success in enrolling drop-outs in evening school programs or in full-time training in technical schools, radio and television schools, nursing schools, and business schools. Both the above-mentioned programs are in process of being evaluated.

One type of enterprise in finding employment is illustrated

by an arrangement the Newark, New Jersey, schools have made with a large department-store chain. All the stores of this chain make employment available, as job vacancies occur, to suitable high school juniors and seniors who are likely to leave school or have already dropped out. It is a condition of employment that the youth remain in school and maintain satisfactory grades. After graduation the youth is eligible for a special training program in the retailing business, which includes such trades as carpentry, painting, baking, typing, policing, advertising, cooking and dietetic work, as well as clerking.[27]

Various other programs designed to combine job training with actual induction into the business world could be cited. For example, there is the Chicago program, with support from the Ford Foundation and Carson Pirie Scott Company. An experiment headed by a professor of landscape architecture at the University of Pennsylvania employs teenagers to build playgrounds, the youth corps involved having been granted "first demolition rights" on renewal projects. The Detroit job-upgrading program under the auspices of the schools and the Youth Service Counsel provides temporary employment for drop-outs in a variety of concerns, with some prospect of more permanent positions. The Rockland County, New York, public school system has been distinctly forward in planning for the various needs of its pupils and its employment-training program is a good example. Training is to a large extent done on the actual job. Student carpenters, plumbers, and sheet-metal workers build houses and youth centers and work on school properties. They have even built a hospital for crippled children. Cooks prepare banquets. Beauty-culture students work for paying clients. Moreover, the program has received full cooperation from local trade unions. Union members have counseled students, helped some get jobs, and found qualified teachers for the training process. The unions have even given considerable financial help and have offered union initiation fees as prizes for successful students. A preapprenticeship experiment is being undertaken under a Brick Masonry Joint Apprenticeship Committee.

High school students showed enough capacity to lay brick and tile true to the line to prove that by school-leaving age they were fit to enter regular apprenticeships.

So effective a liaison between school and job is exceptional and though it sets an excellent example it would not be feasible under less favorable conditions. The policy of combining work experience with schooling, for youths who are not qualified or not minded to proceed to college, is one that deserves wide experimentation, as H. Dillon has pleaded in his book, *Work Experience in Secondary Schools.*[28]

If we look at the problem of post-school employment as a whole, we must conclude that its magnitude is growing and that, although some promising initiatives are developing, far greater and more coordinated measures are needed if it is to be met to any important extent. The school has its own primary role but the concerted efforts of the community, as well as of local, state, and federal governments are also required. In the community, the private employer all the way down to the householder, can be activated to provide additional temporary jobs for youths, for there are always tasks that remain to be done and opportunities that are not taken. The municipality can utilize drop-outs and other unemployed teenagers to do some needed jobs. For example, cities have neighborhood conservation and urban renewal projects, but often enough these accomplish only a fraction of what needs to be done. There is still much more to be done in the training and organizing of unemployed youth to help the restoration process in their own neighborhoods—most of them live in the dilapidated deteriorating areas. Some state governments and the federal government have training programs for teenagers, domestic Peace Corps programs, programs of financial aid, and so forth.

The problem is worthy of every effort that can be made to solve it. Unemployment is highest in the teenage group and is twice as high among the disprivileged minority groups. The costs of inaction or inadequate action are extremely serious. An unemployed youngster loses aspiration, loses incentive, loses hope, and drifts too often into criminal ways. There is no waste that can compare with the waste of the promise, the vitality, and the spirit of youth.

Our concern here is with what the school can do. The changes in the industrial system are spurring our schools to fill a role of preparation for the world of work that in the past has been given too little attention. Our vocational schools serve a purpose, particularly in the training of technicians, but they by no means meet the present need. Under some conditions the system established in the Rockland County schools might, with some further developments, suffice. But, in our great cities where the unemployment of youth has the worst consequences, another approach is more feasible and is imperatively needed.

In our Juvenile Delinquency Education Project (Final Report No. 3) we advocated a branching of the school curriculum into two divisions applicable to pupils around the age of fourteen.[29] Students who show the necessary attributes and are for the most part likely to go on to college or to professional schools of any kind would carry on with a regular academic curriculum. Students who show relatively little interest in or aptitude for academic learning would enter a work-experience division. Both types of students would attend the same schools, and care should be taken to avoid the suggestion that any stigma is attached to entrance into the second division. There might, however, be some schools in which the great majority of the students would belong to the first division, in which case arrangements might be made to locate the minority elsewhere.

Most of the less advanced and more school-shy pupils would go into the second division, which would be equipped with the tools and mechanisms of a variety of trades, and the first task of the teacher would be to discover the respective attitudes and inclinations of the entrants, for it is an exceedingly rare youth who has no work-play interest of any kind. The academic part of the curriculum would be related to the kind of job to which the youth was assigned. Often enough the practical need to know better in order to do better creates an interest in acquiring the necessary knowledge. The school would help to place the pupils in jobs when they finished school, and would maintain contact with many kinds of business for this purpose, as well as to arrange for part-time jobs in the process of learning.

As things are at present, considerable numbers of teenagers in the later years of schooling regard school as a grievous compulsion. When they do not break away altogether they merely waste their time and develop resistances and frustrations. At a meeting of school superintendents at which the writer was present it was agreed that up to 25 per cent of school youth over fourteen get little or no benefit from their schooling. Training that would prepare a future for them would be more congenial and at the same time would help to evoke or revive an incentive for remaining in school that now is wholly lacking. A recent Secretary of Labor proposed that the states should extend the period of compulsory schooling to the age of eighteen. This proposal is in our judgment highly dubious—after seventeen those who are going to college or professional schools should be ready to go, and for the others it would mean an additional year of boredom and revulsion. If the proposal were to be considered at all, it should apply only to those of the work-experience group who remained unemployed.

Summation and General Recommendations

The school is the only agency specifically organized to impart the knowledge and the skills required to equip a child for the business of adult living and also for participation in the scientific and cultural heritage of mankind. It is no substitute for other agencies that also are engaged in the upbringing of the child—the family, the church, the peer group, and the agencies of communication—but it provides training by a professional staff working continuously over many years and is often the only agency with the opportunity and presumably the qualifications to observe with unprejudiced eyes the troubles, the problems, and the needs of the child.

Hence its importance, not only in the teaching but also in the guidance of youth. Its function is to educate, but to fulfill that function it must endeavor to remove the roadblocks to education that fall within the competence of the teachers and to refer to professional therapists those other disturbances that lie beyond his competence.

Bearing these considerations in mind we regard the following recommendations as expressions of some primary obligations of the school system.

1. Since the earlier the child's learning problems are observed, recognized, and treated the better the chance of overcoming them, every school should establish a thoroughgoing early-identification program, beginning with kindergarten. Such a program might indeed be extended with considerable advantage into the preschool programs that are now developing.

2. All teachers should be trained, in their preparation for teaching or in in-service training, to identify problem children and to provide preliminary help and guidance through sympathetic understanding of their needs.

3. All schools should have available specially trained guidance counselors to whom more difficult cases should be referred.

4. To make this service possible, classes should, whenever possible, be limited to twenty or twenty-five pupils, and for particularly refractory or difficult groups to fifteen.

5. A far more intensive effort is essential for the proper instruction of disprivileged groups, particularly the in-migrant groups in urban centers, in order to help them adjust to the conditions of city life and overcome the educational deficiencies of their background. This is of high importance for their future as citizens and directly to prevent their lapsing into delinquent habits.

6. In substandard poverty-stricken urban areas the school cannot operate effectively as an educational agency unless it becomes a neighborhood institution, cooperating with the families of the area and the local welfare organizations and providing special services for the children in order to equip them for schooling. No less imperative is the need to anticipate the likelihood that certain pupils will become drop-outs, and to give special consideration to their needs and their

difficulties, and to stimulate their families through friendly contacts to encourage them to remain in school.

7. For older pupils who have either no interest or too little ability to incline them to continue with the regular academic curriculum, it is eminently desirable that the school have a division providing work-experience courses directly related to the types of jobs on which they have a reasonable chance of being employed.

8. The schools in this country cannot rise to the high demand and challenge involved in the education of the young, and in the special and individual guidance that is the best assurance that children will overcome their difficulties and not fall into delinquent ways, unless the community comes to their aid and enables them to raise their standards, the qualifications required of teachers, the salary rates, and the whole status of the profession.

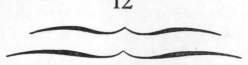

Inclusive Neighborhood and Community Programs

Since delinquency on any scale stems from a complex of conditions, programs that view the problem as a many-sided one and attack it concertedly from different angles deserve special consideration. The number of such programs now in process of development reveals the growth of a better understanding of the causes of delinquency. An additional spur to this more intelligent approach is the spectacle of massive riots by Negro youth in the slums of Los Angeles, New York, and other cities, creating serious damage, loss of life, and grave disturbances of the public order. Whatever immediate incitements may have touched off these explosive outbursts, they could not have occurred except for the pent-up anger and misery of a population suffering grievous ills and rankling from a sense of social injustice. We have already insisted that so long as ghettolike slums exist the frustration of the youth inhabiting them will find an outlet in delinquency. At the same time much can be done to rescue the youth of such areas by providing for them the aid, training, equipment, and work opportunities available to more fortunately placed youths. Such programs must be organized and developed on a neighborhood or district basis, in order to achieve the necessary close-up relationships with the group, but it is for the larger community to provide the major resources and to ensure that they are applied with due regard to the needs and interests of the group they serve.

The lack of comprehensive planning to meet the problems of troubled and disoriented youth has been a main weakness in the strategy of delinquent prevention. Different agencies have sought to deal with it, each from its own viewpoint, without coordination. Many family service agencies have limited their effectiveness because they have not viewed the family as a whole, have not dealt with the often difficult relationships between parents and youth or have not reacted to the background troubles of youth that disturb these relationships, or have followed some particular social-work methodology that narrowed their approach.[1] A review of twenty-one selected social programs showed that ten followed a group-work method and six a casework method, while only two were oriented to an all-around approach.[2]

Employment-focused Programs

Some of the newer, more inclusive programs focus round one particular objective but include various others, realizing that the initial aim can be reached only by dealing with a whole series of impediments that block its achievement. Foremost among these are programs geared to providing work-opportunities for disprivileged youth. Unemployment is exceptionally high among this group, and those who are employed have for the most part casual and badly paid jobs that lead nowhere. They lack incentive because there's little to hope for and whether they become sullen or rough-riding they are alike in danger of becoming demoralized and delinquent. Whatever else may be done to help such youth is not likely to be effective unless they are given some assurance of a future, something to occupy their time that promises betterment and advancement. Work opportunity is therefore a primary requisite. But this implies realistic training, new contacts and associations, the removal of educational deficiencies, some instruction in manners and in modes of speech, recreational facilities for their free time, not infrequently better living conditions, temporary support, work-training programs, and aid in placement. Work opportunity becomes the focus of a comprehensive program.

The most extensive of such programs is being developed under the Manpower and Training Act, which concentrates on the training of youth in areas where there is considerable youth unemployment, the congested urban areas of Chicago, St. Louis, Detroit, Washington, Los Angeles, Boston, Milwaukee, New York, and other cities. The youth enlisted under this program range from sixteen to twenty-two years of age. Various government agencies combine in the development of the training program. The older youth receive allowances up to $20 per week, and the public employment offices devote themselves to the placement of those who have completed their training in some particular trade or skill.[3]

A good example of a local program largely focused on employment is the New Haven Manpower Program, a major area of the all-around system of welfare projects presided over by that city through Community Progress, Inc. While it offers a unified service of training, guidance, and general aid for those who are in need of vocational education, education in industrial arts, apprenticeship opportunities, and so forth, working in close cooperation with a considerable variety of agencies, it also has special services for those with serious educational deficiencies and for the counseling of out-of-school youth, disprivileged minority-group youth, and unemployed youngsters generally. It operates on the neighborhood level, with the aid of neighborhood services, and plans to give the schools a central place in the community life. Associated with it is a retraining committee made up of leading employers and educators who provide retraining facilities geared to the special conditions of the New Haven labor market. Besides furnishing specific training in many fields, the program is also concerned with the broader educational qualifications so often lacking among the unemployed and the unskilled, and finally it gives some consideration to the social problems of the out-of-work, including the problem of delinquency.[4]

Among its various operations New Haven takes particular note of the need to provide leisure-time activities. On the basis of a four-year study jointly sponsored by the Citizens Action

Commission and the Community Council of Greater New Haven a project has been formulated which includes clubs and lounges and entertainments, as well as general recreation facilities, and also counseling services especially directed to delinquent and out-of-school youth. These provisions will be set up, with the aid of neighborhood volunteers, in neighborhoods where the need is greatest. The whole project is remarkably thorough and well designed. The addition of leisure-time facilities for teen-agers is no mere frill; such facilities can be a significant factor in the redirection of the activities and energies of disoriented and delinquent youth.

No city has realized more effectively than has New Haven the fact that insulated attacks on individual problems within the complex of urban slum conditions that cramp the energies and distort the aspirations of youth are likely to be futile, over-weighted by the pressures of the environment and the habits and attitudes they engender. New Haven has apparently succeeded in embracing within an integrated plan not only the resources available in the city itself but also contributions from the state as well as a program for families in public housing provided by the Department of Health, Education and Welfare. If the execution of this embracing project is worthy of its planning it could be-come a model for the treatment of our most grievous urban ills. The much-needed coordination of welfare services is also be-ginning to be recognized and pursued in a number of other cities, including Chicago, with its Joint Youth Development Program; Oakland, California, with its Inter-Agency Project; St. Louis with its Gateways for Youth; and Boston with its three multi-service centers.[5]

School-focused Programs

The school is an obvious neighborhood institution around which a broad plan of local welfare services can be organized. It plays an important role in many inclusive programs, not least in the New Haven one. In fact, it is merely for convenience of classification that we place here some of the major developments of inclusive community service. Some schools or school systems have independently provided services for the families of their pupils; others have broadened their in-school services to help make good the social and cultural deficiencies of pupils in deteriorated neighborhoods. The All-Day Neighborhood Schools of the New York City Board of Education are an admirable example of the first type of service and the Higher Horizons program falls into the second type.[6] Those engaged in developing guidance programs of schools in various areas have realized that they must work with the families of their pupils if they are to deal at all successfully with the problems that interfere with the children's education. The Ford Foundation has launched various programs to develop extra school-based services, such as remedial training and expanded guidance facilities in difficult schools.

In the Chicago Joint Youth Development Program the role of the school is pivotal in a program that includes also a wide range of community services, health, housing, employment, recreation, law enforcement, etc. Specific projects are being formulated to meet the need of localities and of special problem groups. Neighborhood activities will center around the neighborhood schools. A lookout is to be kept for signs of behavioral disturbance and vulnerability to juvenile delinquency. The school doors are open to citizens who can drop in at any time and present their problems. Short-term counseling is to be immediately available, and long-term counseling for those who have serious troubles will be provided through a special unit. Demonstration projects of various kinds are under consideration, and special efforts will be made to bridge the departmentalization that has so often obstructed the efficiency of the various services.[7]

Another school-oriented program is in progress in the Benneker elementary school district of St. Louis. Its primary objective is to stimulate the children of this impoverished, predominantly Negro area to better scholastic achievement. This endeavor called for cooperation by various social and philanthropic organizations. It has required a revision of attitudes among teachers and principals who needed a new approach to the potentialities of their retarded pupils, as well as special training for social workers employed in the schools. And it has called regular meetings with parents to discuss their problems, to aid them in their troubles, and to enlist their help in the effort to raise the sights of the children. Thoroughgoing support from the whole community is essential, if the school is to accomplish its vital but sometimes apparently impossible function of educating the children of our depressed urban areas.[8]

Inclusive Regional Programs

For convenience we place here some broad-based projects that take for their province a distinctive urban area, considerably larger than a neighborhood, in which a high rate of delinquency is but one of a crowding number of social ills. The most notable of such projects are Haryou-Act, located in central Harlem, and Mobilization for Youth, covering the Lower East Side of Manhattan.[9] Both operate on quite a large scale and possess funds which enable them to carry on an unusual number of concerted activities. But each has various characteristics peculiar to itself.

Haryou-Act (Harlem Youth Opportunities Unlimited in conjunction with Associated Community Teams) is confronted with what may well be the most aggravated concentration of social troubles to be found in any urban area of the United States. In this Negro ghetto long-time exploitation and discrimination are being met with the aroused passions of a bewildered population in whom the new urge for liberation has largely replaced an old apathy. Of all the Health Center districts in New York City, Harlem stands highest in the indices for sociopathological factors, for health afflictions, for economic deprivation and dependence, and for juvenile delinquency. Narcotic addiction is an increasing threat in the area. A heroic enterprise will be required to convert its wretched housing and hemmed-in congestion to decent living conditions.

Haryou has to gear its manifold activities to conditions that make its every operation more difficult. For example, in its educational work it cannot be content merely with advancing programs for raising the standards of the school pupils. It must press for the reconstruction and renovation of the schools themselves, while there is also much controversy over the question whether and how Harlem pupils should be redistributed within the greater school system. More directly, it is faced with the excessive retardation and the inefficient previous schooling of so many of these children. To meet these problems it has set up a system of preschool preparation and intensive measures for remedial work to make up educational backwardness, as well as a special academy for the sixteen-to-seventeen group, and practical and cultural workshops of various kinds. In this endeavor it is receiving considerable support from City and State authorities. It has also become a special beneficiary under the Federal Anti-Poverty Program.

Again, Harlem not only has a high proportion of youthful delinquents and parolees returning from the custodial training schools, but also is an area to which certain undesirable characters, including dope peddlers, gravitate. Incidentally, there is some reason to suspect that the Negro youth is less protected than the white youth and more liable to arrest for minor offenses. There is a strong sentiment in the area that the police for the most part are particularly harsh with Negroes caught in any trouble. Whatever degree of justification there may have been for this feeling in the past, it is satisfactory to know that the police authorities are now seeking to establish better relationships. This is certainly an area in which the young are exposed to particular dangers and need a helping hand at every turn. To meet this situation Haryou-Act has devised various expedients, including a Cadet Corps and an Adult Volunteers Corps. Efforts are made to enable the young to associate with good citizens and to give them training in citizenship. There is also a special arrangement to give young people released from institutions the protection and friendly support which they need at the stage of their return. Since unemployment is abnormally high among urban Negro youth, vocational training and job placement are given special consideration.

Among the crowding troubles of the area is the final resort of drug addiction. To counter this a special project has been devised which includes, on the one hand, a drive on dope peddlers and the centers of distribution of narcotics, and, on the other, facilities for detoxification and rehabilitation in a fully equipped upstate institution. The provision of after-care—often desperately lacking—is a special concern, in an effort to protect former addicts and integrate them with the life and work of the community.

The Harlem program is a remarkable enterprise, but it has been beset by formidable difficulties, conflicting interests, and galling reminders of the gulf between plans and achievements. There is also the stubborn problem, which is mainly beyond its power, of eliminating slum conditions over a large area which has been allowed to deteriorate to the lowest point and which is further blocked by social resistance to the free movement of Negroes into other residential areas.

Haryou has from the very beginning encountered serious embarrassments because of conflicts between local controls, direct or indirect, and the program directors and operative staff. The first director resigned after a few months, the second after a considerably longer period of frustrating experience. At the time of writing Haryou is again in a crisis, owing to charges of lax bookkeeping and other complaints, which an official committee is currently assessing. It would be peculiarly unfortunate if so vital an enterprise, in an area where the need for it is maximum, an enterprise on a scale never achieved before and one with adequate financing, were to be mutilated by power struggles and its promise to inaugurate a new era for the people of Harlem and its grossly unregarded youth defeated.

Our second example, Mobilization for Youth, presents some striking contrasts to the Harlem project.[10] It is situated in a less desperate area, the Lower East Side of Manhattan, an area that has been changing considerably with the influx of Puerto Ricans and other in-migrant groups. This area is a troubled one, with many social problems, including gang fighting and a rather high delinquency rate. But it has better local resources than has

Harlem, including several superior social settlements, from one of which, Henry Street, the project was initiated, and an effective Lower East Side Neighborhood Association. The project has accordingly received highly competent support and neighborhood cooperation. It has strong financial resources, the major amount coming from several federal agencies, with very considerable City aid as well as a grant from the Ford Foundation. While in a broad way it serves the whole area, it is oriented primarily to the provision of opportunities and amenities for the young and is especially concerned to aid in the prevention of delinquency. The success it may register in the latter respect should be a good index of the success of the whole program.

More explicitly than most projects in this field, Mobilization for Youth has formulated its philosophy and its plan of operation.[11] In the first place it holds the lower economic group to be grossly underserved by the voluntary welfare agencies in general. A recent study of family agencies has shown that they provide more service to those with high school and college education than to the less well educated. In other words, where the need is greatest, the service is least. Part of the reason is that the poorer and less educated are less prepared to communicate their problems and seek assistance. They feel ill at ease in dealing with agencies which seem remote from them, whose staffs have a language unlike their own ways of speech, and which frequently require the filling in of complicated forms. MFY endeavors in its own servicing to bridge this gap. It sets up, wherever feasible, organizations of its own, Youth Job Centers, the Youth Adventure Corps, its Neighborhood Service Center, its Training Department, with rooms for meetings, coffee shops, and so forth.

Within its wide range of projects, MFY gives training for work opportunities a central place. It has its own workshops, where it trains youths in carpentry, masonry, painting, cooking, waiting at tables, sewing and the making of children's clothes, clerical and office work, automobile repairs. It uses a Shell Oil station, and places trainees at Beth Israel Hospital as aides and orderlies. The importance of these operations may be better realized when we learn that approximately 50 per cent of its clientele are Puerto Ricans and the Negro enrollment runs from 25 to 30 per cent. These are the youths who have the greatest difficulty in finding work, whose education has been least advanced, and who lack the practical training for decent jobs. In the earlier stages between 15 and 20 per cent dropped out of the program, but careful counseling brought half of these back. For those with special disabilities, physical or mental, special therapy is sought.

On-the-job training is being provided, on a subsidized basis, as an expedient for skill-upgrading. Employers are paid up to $30 a week for the trainees so that the latter may be paid the standard labor rate. This program, however, has been questioned, because of reservations about its effectiveness. One issue is whether the schools should not provide work-training programs rather than academic ones for older youngsters in grades 7 to 9, who otherwise might be wasting their time at school or becoming drop-outs. In our JDEP report on New York City Schools we made a plea for this proposal.

Through a variety of expedients MFY endeavors to deal with the people on their own terms, eschewing the jargon of social work and communicating in the language of the folk. It seeks to make its neighborhood associations as autonomous as possible. It employs indigenous personnel in a large variety of staff positions, as visiting homemakers, parent-education aides, case aides, group leaders, coffee-shop managers, and others. Its meeting places are homey—you can walk right in from the street and you don't need an appointment. It consults youthful attitudes and styles in providing leisure-time recreations and facilities. Its Adventure Corps, for example, has some of the trappings of a military outfit, with drill and banners and parades.

The professional staff keeps a watchful eye on operations but intervenes as little as possible. It sets standards and directions and allows room for trial and error on the part of the local associations. Obviously, it is responsible for the management of the funds that make the associations possible but it encourages self-help in the community. In short, it wants to make the community feel that the new facilities and services are their own and that all are working together for the future of the community's young people.

In spite of its manifest services, MFY's policy of allowing the groups it serves to give free vent to their attitudes, complaints, and reactions to existing conditions has brought it into serious trouble. Some small element of its clientele, using the facilities of MFY, circulated damning indictments of the *status quo*. There was a hue and cry, with charges that MFY was fostering subversives. We agree that the organization might have been more alert to control such manifestations, especially in view of the temper of the times. There were also complaints of extravagant expenditures. Both charges appear to have been grossly magnified, but there was danger that this signal and pioneering enterprise would be undermined by the violent attacks of those who do not understand either the fine service it is rendering or the clamant need for it. However, some new controls were established, and MFY appears now to be developing and improving its range of service.

Both Haryou and MFY have received substantial new grants under the Federal Anti-Poverty Program and will thus be in a position to broaden considerably their range of operations.

The three types of community-oriented programs we have thus far considered by no means exhaust the ways in which such programs can be instituted or organized. Any particular social objective for the welfare of youth can be broadened into a range of operations that takes on a community character. Any social institution or movement can make itself a center that plans and coordinates an integrated series of many-sided social activities. The logic of service prompts all-round programs, since the achievement of any one objective, such as the reduction of juvenile delinquency, involves remedial activities in a variety of directions. A project may begin with, say, the provision of recreation or entertainment, but its directors will soon find that the youth thus served have many problems that interfere with its efforts. The focus of community service may thus be a playground association, a neighborhood house or settlement, or a police precinct.

Again, the coverage of the program may not be a region or larger community but a small neighborhood. A program on this lesser scale is feasible with quite limited resources and may serve as a pilot project for a series of similar programs. Various attempts have been made to set up such neighborhood centers. The writer was responsible for the planning of one in a high-delinquency neighborhood in the South Bronx, New York City, while he was director of the City's Juvenile Delinquency Evaluation Project. As our investigation proceeded, we were more and more impressed with the fact that while large sums were being spent on the rehabilitation of conscious delinquents, with at best only a modicum of success, very little was being done to reach incipient delinquents and "vulnerable" youths, at the stage where the chances of reform or change of direction were far greater. Accordingly, with some additional funds received through the intervention of Abe Stark, then President of the Council, we chose a fairly well-demarcated neighborhood and planted within it a small professional staff. The inhabitants were organized through a neighborhood committee and neighborhood volunteers were enlisted. A beginning was made in the enlistment of block captains who would be in a position to report on any youngsters who needed our aid, counsel, or support in any way. We established excellent relations with the South Bronx Community Council, with the neighborhood public schools, and with various neighborhood welfare agencies, while a church in the neighborhood was especially cooperative. We found quickly, however, that the cordial support of the people of the neighborhood was more readily secured if we sought to serve them in other ways. The great majority were Puerto Ricans, recent in-migrants, who were without experience in dealing with officials. They sought our help when they had complaints about housing violations or trouble with the Department of Welfare, or schooling difficulties, and so forth. We set up quite a variety of services—for young mothers, for children in need, for after-school play facilities, for pupils whose English was inadequate. As a result we won their confidence and were freely consulted about troubled or difficult children. Not infrequently children themselves came to us with their problems. Our little professional group situated in the neighborhood became integrated into the neighborhood.

Comments and Conclusions

The strategic advantage of a unified centrally directed program over a series of separate single-objective operations, one devoted, say, to delinquency, one to health problems, one to employment training and placement, and so forth, should be obvious, especially in dealing with neighborhoods or groups suffering from serious handicaps. If delinquents are our primary concern, we have to do something about their schooling, about their associations, about their home life, about their opportunities for jobs, and sometimes about their health conditions. If unemployment is the problem we are attacking, obviously the chances of decent employment depend on training in the appropriate skills, a respectable general education, decent manners, good work habits, and the ability to get along with others. We could go further and say that every single welfare objective is advanced by advances made in all other welfare objectives. Every gain in one direction sustains a gain in other directions. If, for example, you improve the probation system, some youngsters will receive the friendly counsel and aid and new associations they badly need, which may save them from being institutionalized, may mean the restoration of family relationships, may mean they make better grades at school, may mean they are referred for some health service, and so forth. A beneficent cycle of changes may be substituted for a vicious circle.

The integration of the various operations of an inclusive community program, so that they are all geared together with adequate understanding among the various areas of operation, is a task calling for high capacity and expertise in the director. In some cases, irrelevant considerations in the choice of a director or the unwillingness to search for and adequately compensate effective leadership has militated against the success of community programs that otherwise were well designed.

The various community programs we have described are

mostly in the initial or developing stage. They cannot therefore be evaluated at present by the only sure test, that of actual results. We have suggested that integrated programs have the potentiality of much greater impact on the many-sided problems of youth, and it is therefore of high importance that continuing research be built into them, leading up to final evaluations. Some of these programs are taking steps in this direction. The Chicago program, for example, contemplates a series of studies to analyze the direct impact of its various operations and also to interpret the significance of its united attack. New Haven plans to test the working of the actual techniques it employs in the several areas, the effect of the coordination of operations on the quality and effectiveness of service, and the relative availability of qualified workers in various social welfare fields.

In sum, the following are our conclusions respecting the strategy of inclusive programs.

1. Since delinquency, like many other social ills, takes various forms and results from the combined impact of a complex of adverse conditions, the attack on it should also be many-sided, the different lines being geared into an integrated program.

2. The locus of operation should be the neighborhood, to assure close relations between the people and the operating staff, and the whole field of action should be a reasonably well-demarcated region.

3. A many-sided program is likely to gain in concentration and efficacy if it gives a central place to some one important problem, say education for employment (social as well as academic and technical), and if it can focus its activities in each neighborhood around an appropriate school or community center.

4. The experience of Haryou and Mobilization for Youth emphasizes the need that such major regional organizations, financed from governmental and private sources, be actively supervised by a highly qualified body, composed of welfare specialists, social scientists, and area representatives. Such a body should not be empowered to prescribe policies and methods of operation but should make evaluative comments

and suggestions and would be able to defend the organization against unwarranted attacks. It would also be desirable that a small committee of research experts be employed part time to keep in close touch with program developments, assess results, and make proposals to the director for operative improvements.

13

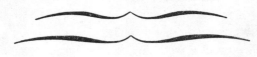

The Police

The police constitute the first line of defense against juvenile delinquency. As such and as the petitioners in the cases of four out of five young persons referred to the juvenile courts, the police largely determine the extent to which the behavior deviations of young people in any community will be officially registered. About one million children a year are estimated to have contact with the police. More than three times as many juveniles under the age of eighteen as appear before the juvenile courts of the country come to the attention of police agencies, according to a United States Children's Bureau estimate. This is more than eight times the number placed in detention and ten times the number put on probation by the courts.[1]

The police officer may resort to one of several alternatives with troublesome children. He may deem a warning sufficient or he may decide upon a referral to a juvenile court or a community agency. In some communities responsibility for the redirection of the less serious offenders is personally assumed by the officer. The individual officer's discretion and training and the availability of alternative services for the young persons' care will largely determine his decision in the exercise of the responsibility assigned to him by the community. His individual discretion to warn, apprehend, detain, or refer a child to juvenile court considerably governs a police officer's decision within the dictates of official regulation.

Most of the cases handled in the initial contact appear relatively simple. The majority come to the police department's official attention only once, for a curfew violation, pilfering, bullying, or a prank, for instance. Quite often this will be the family's only contact with the police department in a lifetime. Whether this contact is well advised or rough and shabby is most important in creating an attitude toward police authority.

While a sizable proportion of police referrals probably arise from community complaint, Alfred J. Kahn points out that in New York City an overwhelming majority of the non-arrest cases referred to the Investigation Unit come through the police.[2] More alleged delinquents and children in trouble have their first official contact with the Police Youth Division than with all other agencies put together. More than half of all children reported to the New York City Youth Board in 1955 were known to the Juvenile Aid Bureau of the Police Department. There are comparable findings in other cities. About 30 to 40 per cent involve only a precautionary letter, and a third are referred to the parents following home investigation. Of the remainder, many have previous records and are handled in the courts or in social agencies. In New York City about 2,000 new referrals to court and social agencies emerge out of some 34,000 non-arrest cases annually.

Various sources bring juveniles to the notice of the police, including complaints from outside observers who witnessed some violation or made some direct surveillance. A study by G. A. Mitchell disclosed that the bases on which officers of the Youth Bureau of the Detroit Police Department decided, during an initial contact with a boy on the street, whether to handle the case formally or informally were somewhat loose.[3] If the family seemed to the officer to be interested in the boy and if the home was neat, the case tended to be handled informally. Children of "above average" intelligence had a good chance of being referred to an agency. If a boy was respectful to the officer and cooperative he stood a good chance of being released. A boy large for his age was regarded as a likely trouble-maker. "I refer most big boys to court," said one officer.

The police officer's role in this respect is to distinguish between the offender for whom a warning is sufficient and the more serious delinquent. To do so, he should have some understanding of the problems and troubles of children. In addition to information about juvenile court law and protective obligations in neglect cases, he should have enough knowledge of social agencies and community resources to direct people in need or in trouble. He should be instructed in the rights of young people during the questioning and other phases of investigation and in the conditions under which resort to detention facilities is desirable.

The activities of the police in dealing with juveniles should center round a specially trained section of the police department—its bureau for juveniles. The average policeman is not qualified to deal on his own with troublesome children, and the nature of his task in contact with criminals tends to develop attitudes that are not propitious for such dealings. All policemen should certainly be given a general training in the way to handle children, but with the scale of the police force such training can only be of a screening character. The special youth unit should be quite distinct. Its members should be selected on a different basis, from young persons with special aptitudes. In the New York City juvenile bureau and some others most of the members have college degrees in relevant subjects. In some areas police training for juvenile work is done in collaboration with colleges and universities. This important development is exhibited in the Federal Bureau of Investigation's educational activities at the National Police Academy, which has inaugurated preservice police training programs, pioneered by August Volmer and now regularly scheduled at nearly a dozen colleges and universities. Another significant example is the Delinquency Control Institute under the direction of the School of Public Administration at the University of Southern California, which is regarded as having a quite effective impact in California generally, as well as in other western states.[4]

The Police College now established under the aegis of the Board of Higher Education for the instruction of the New York City police force is also a signal advance beyond the earlier

Police Academy. But in most communities, except for a few great cities, police provision for dealing with the young is wholly inadequate. The imperative importance of such provision is better appreciated if we realize that the function of the police is not only to suppress law-breaking but to prevent it. And when dealing with youngsters the preventive function is paramount. Sir Robert Peel, who in the early nineteenth century reorganized the London police force (who are called "bobbies" to this day), maintained that the primary responsibility of the force is to prevent crime and public disorder, not simply to arrest the criminal. The police guard children when crossing streets to school, bring the young ones home when they stray and direct and warn children in various situations. It is their task also to direct and warn them away from law violation, and since they are usually the first officials who are in contact with children, they have unusual opportunties to perform this essential service. But to do so they need to be educated in the ways and needs of children as well as in the requirements of the law.

All cases of young persons who show signs of having serious problems or of being seriously disturbed or difficult, and all in which there is a record of previous offenses, should be referred from the regular police to the special youth unit, and all policemen should be instructed in the symptoms that call for the service of a trained youth staff. It should indeed be a general principle that, wherever feasible, the special youth police officer is called at an early stage to dispose of and to process juvenile cases. This special unit should decide whether a case should go directly before the court or whether some preliminary program of investigation or referral is requisite.

Not only should the training of the youth bureau personnel be distinctive but so should their social responsibilities. Their mission should include the patrolling and inspection of places and premises that attract youth, and especially juvenile hangouts of dubious character. They should take the lead in establishing, for the police in general, good working relationships with welfare agencies and civic associations. Saul Bernstein, in his recent survey, *Youth on the Streets,* found that the part played by the police juvenile bureaus was of primary importance in the maintenance of good understanding between the police and the social agency workers with whom they come into contact.[5] The cooperation of welfare agencies with the police and vice versa can be highly advantageous to both.

Of no less significance is the cooperation between the police and the schools. The particularly difficult or disturbed pupils who give so much concern to teachers are not unlikely to come also to the attention of the police, and the teachers can provide a far more intelligent report on them than outsiders or even members of the children's families can give. Such information is more significant if it is conveyed to policemen who have the requisite training, and that for the most part means members of the juvenile bureau. A close working relationship between the police and the school can be the means of avoiding serious errors in treatment.

An illustration is provided from a report on police-school liaison in Flint, Michigan.[6] During the period 1958–1959, in the area where the liaison program was operating, only one out of every 280 public school students was involved in a crime, as compared with one in every 36 such students outside the area. In the city as a whole there were 200 repeaters, whereas in the program district there were none. Even making allowance for the diverse conditions of the various city districts this was a remarkable showing.

The need for concentrated service on the part of the police juvenile unit in areas where there is tension between different ethnic groups has been highlighted by recent happenings in a number of large cities. Frequently in such areas open conflict between opposing groups is initiated by undisciplined youths or again by youths seething with anger against what they regard as gross injustice or discrimination. There are also not infrequent outbreaks that are triggered by resentment against what is regarded as needless violence or brutality on the part of the police, especially when they are seeking to make an arrest. So far has this spirit spread in certain areas in New York City that even the action of the police in arresting a youth who has committed a serious offense may cause a riot. Recently this attitude has been so pronounced in Puerto Rican areas that the police authorities have instituted a special program designed to give the police who move in these areas a more friendly and sympathetic relation to Puerto Ricans. A party of police were even sent to Puerto Rico to help improve this understanding. From first reports the program would seem to have been beneficial.

Negroes are particularly prone to the belief that the police treat them with more roughness and lack of consideration than they show to other groups. Certainly some very bad outbreaks of violence have occurred in the course of police contacts with Negro youth. One of the worst and most sustained riots in Harlem was caused by the fatal shooting of a youth who was forcefully resisting a police arrest. Since the policeman in question was exonerated by the police authorities after a hearing of the case, the event gave impetus to a demand that charges of police brutality or violence be heard by a civilian body.

The New York City Police Department has recently become much concerned over the hostile attitudes so frequently manifested by Negro and Puerto Rican groups toward the police, and is making concerted efforts to remedy the situation, both through police training and through the education of the public concerning the problems faced by the police. To advance this policy the Police College is preparing, under a Ford Foundation grant, a police training film, dealing primarily with the relations between the police and the community.

Members of the juvenile bureau could be especially helpful in spotting locations of rising tensions, probing the causes of tensions, recognizing the incitements that trigger youth uprisings, and reporting to the authorities. They would enlist the aid of strategically located persons, including school teachers, community workers, and Negro leaders, and they themselves would be more effective in dealings with the youthful disturbers than the regular police are likely to be. Their role would be not to substitute for the regular police but to cooperate with them.

Another activity entrusted to the police calls for both understanding of youth problems and knowledge of the capacities of available social agencies. This is the matter of referrals, especially referrals in cases where the offense is deemed not to require, in the first instance, court handling. We have observed that many cases referred to agencies are never followed through. The agency may be already overloaded. Sometimes a perfunctory home call is made and receives no response and the case is marked "closed." Often the final comment on the agency record is simply "did not cooperate."[7] The selection of an agency should be discriminating and the communication with it fully informative, and there should always be a follow-up to find out what, if anything, has been done. The trained juvenile unit officer is best qualified to undertake this task.

Again, since a large number of juvenile offenses result directly or indirectly from gang associations, the juvenile officer can play a special role through his knowledge of the ways and attitudes of the various kinds of gangs. While the reaction of gang members to the regular police is one of fear and strong aversion, the juvenile officer has a better chance of bringing influence to bear on them. When a whole group of gang members is apprehended—sometimes merely on the charge of "unlawful assembly," sometimes because an offense was committed by one or more members of the group—he is better able to distinguish the guilty members from those who went along simply because of gang allegiance or pressure.

To sum up, since juvenile offenders are distinguished from adult offenders under the laws that set up courts for juveniles, since they are not, except under very special circumstances, regarded as criminals but as wayward youth who need protection, treatment or rehabilitation, the investigation of their cases should also be distinctive: it calls for a particular police division or bureau composed of persons specially trained for the purpose. Experience has shown that such persons are better qualified than the regular police to assess problems of youth and to make recommendations on the disposition of cases. To take one example, in our Juvenile Delinquency Evaluation Project for New York City we studied the court disposition over one year (1955) of the cases that came before the court through the regular police and those that were brought before it by the Juvenile Aid Bureau of the Police Department. Of JAB arrests 24.8 per cent were discharged or dismissed by the Children's Court of that period, as compared with 39.3 per cent of those arrested by the regular police department as a whole.[8] This at least suggests that the screening process of the juvenile officers was more effective, a conclusion that was corroborated by other evidences.

Not infrequently the juvenile bureau is inadequately equipped and undermanned. The service they do or can render is often not properly recognized by the police hierarchy, though there are some fine exceptions. In one situation we studied, the juvenile bureau was a kind of detached body, and there was little if any opportunity for a service career within it. The Children's Bureau's standard calls for a scale of not less than 5 per cent of the total police force and the possession of divisional status.

Conclusions

1. All "beat" policemen should be given instruction not only in the laws and regulations that apply to juveniles but also concerning the types of trouble characteristic of youthful offenders and the manner in which the police should deal with them. They should be taught, with illustrative cases, under what conditions arrests should be made and when specified alternative procedures are to be adopted, as well as when to refer cases to the special juvenile unit.

2. All cities of any scale should have a police bureau or division, well-equipped and adequately manned, to deal with the many cases of troubled youth that come to the attention of the police. Its members should be selected for their ability to establish effective relationships with the young and their capacity to understand and deal with youth problems. In smaller police systems some specially selected policemen should be appointed for this service. There should also be a continuing and comprehensive in-service training program for youth officers.

3. Wherever possible, members of the juvenile unit should be called in to assess and report on the cases of all young people exhibiting serious problems who come to the attention of the "beat" policemen, and they should also be given a

special mission to deal with troublesome gang situations and with situations where youthful groups are fomenting trouble.

4. The juvenile unit should be given full opportunity to maintain close contact with the social agencies to which referrals are made, with the families of trouble-making children, and with the schools.

5. The police on the beat should be carefully trained to show a friendly attitude to the public, especially in areas inhabited by minority or disprivileged groups. The exhibition of bias and intolerance or needless roughness not only alienates the community and discourages public cooperation, but also provokes hostile demonstration and dangerous incidents. The police are the guardians of the people. That is the face they should show to the community.

14

The Court

The juvenile court, said Roscoe Pound, is the greatest forward step in Anglo-American jurisprudence since Magna Charta.[1] It might well have seemed so when one considers the degrading, cruel, and inherently stupid treatment that once was meted out to young people in the name of justice. The new court rejected their treatment as criminals and instead saw them as wards of the court who needed protection, guidance, training, and rehabilitation. It was to be nonpunitive. The offenders before it would have no stigma, no damning record. The findings were to be secret or at least confidential. No reporters could publicize their cases or exhibit their photographs. The only consideration before the court was how best it could assure, within its means, the future welfare of the juveniles.

But in the rough and tumble of political life the shining principle becomes somewhat tarnished. Juvenile court judges are often appointed without regard to their particular qualifications for this special task. The calendars are crowded and the harassed judge has not the time to give the cases before him the careful consideration they may need. The evidence presented by the police officer and the probation officer is often casual, hearsay, superficial, and sketchy. The parents who must appear in court with their offspring are unused to this situation and often tongue-tied or bewildered. Sometimes they are Spanish-speaking, their English is faulty or lacking, and no interpreter is at hand.[2] Counsel is rarely present, although the parents have the right to ask for legal aid. Appeals are rarely made from the court adjudication, since the process is slow and expensive. If the offender is adjudicated, the case may be discharged, often with a warning or some advice from the judge, or the judge may resort to one of two main forms of disposition—probation or commitment to an institution, either a state training school or a custodial institution under private or religious auspices. Probation, which is the resort in a majority of cases, has been in most areas a grossly underdeveloped service, conducted by inadequately trained personnel carrying too heavy caseloads. Custodial treatment carries a serious risk and should not be imposed if a feasible alternative is available. Some judges resort to it with too little consideration, and the courts generally have been slow to recognize the need for diagnostic centers, to which difficult cases could be referred to make advisory reports on disposition.

Most of the nonadjudicated cases are simply dismissed, without any referral, though in some areas of the country they may be put on unofficial probation.

During the period in which we studied the New York City Children's Court (since then incorporated into the Family Court), some 50 per cent of all cases appearing before the judge were either dismissed or discharged. The considerable percentage of cases thus treated in courts across the country, especially in the larger cities, is a sufficient indication that the initial screening system or intake process is either inefficient or is not given enough authority to do a proper job. Some judges hold that it is a salutary experience for a naughty child to confront the court, but this is questionable. In any event with calendars already crowded, the present procedure prevents the judge from giving more serious cases the attention they deserve.

Since probation is the main form of disposition, there is all the more reason why this much neglected service should be given the development of which it is capable. What is needed, in brief, is (1) more efficient recruiting of trained personnel, with adequate salaries to attract them; (2) limitation of the caseload to not more than perhaps 40 cases during any one period; and (3) reorganization of the probation office staff so that it is regarded as a professional service. These are prerequisites for the proper fulfillment of the two main functions of the probation officer: to provide the judge with a discerning report on the youth's background and living conditions and thus to aid him in making the most desirable disposition, and to guide the youth entrusted to his charge into law-abiding habits and associations.

In broad outline, such is the general situation with juvenile courts today. There are some admirable juvenile court judges, and there are a few juvenile court systems that have highly qualified presiding judges. But the general lack of recognition that for this special function judges need special qualifications, the congested court calendars, the lack of adequate screening prior to court appearance, the fact that in most jurisdictions judges spend only part of their time on the juvenile court bench, and the rotation of the job over a panel of judges, all militate against any adequate accomplishment of the great objective for which the juvenile court was designed.

The Desirability of Separating Adjudication from Disposition

There has been considerable questioning of the propriety of the prevailing system which leaves it exclusively to the judge to determine the action to be taken with the adjudicated delinquent. The decision may be crucial for the whole future of the juvenile. For some the commitment to an institution may be in effect a condemnation to a criminal career. Others need special therapy or other service. The judge has not the time and often enough not the knowledge to understand the needs or the various complications of troubled youth. Two alternative methods have been advocated and in some cases have been put into operation. One would entrust the disposition, after the judge has adjudicated the youngster as delinquent, to a specially qualified body. As Professor Alfred Kahn has put it, "It should be possible to devise an administrative structure that permits appropriate delegation of disposition choices to technical specialists without affecting the judge's role as an adjudicator or separating him from the knowledge of the consequences of his decisions."[3] The other method is to have attached to the court a diagnostic center, composed of appropriate experts, to which problem cases would be referred for an advisory report on disposition, leaving the verdict to the court. Both alternatives have the additional advantage that any authority assigned such a task would be very conscious of the inadequacy of the disposition facilities available to the court in most areas and would take a lead in the effort to provide treatment centers, supervised residential facilities, foster homes, short-term testing or diagnostic centers, and other substitutes for the old-style "training school."

A Youth Correctional Authority Act was designed and approved by the American Law Institute as a model for the improvement of the disposition of cases. It calls for a youth authority to which the task would be entrusted. An act along the lines of this model was adopted by California and in one form or another the model has since been followed by four other states— Minnesota, Wisconsin, Texas, and Massachusetts.[4] A few more states, including New Jersey and New York, have made some changes in the same direction.

Under the California plan the court decides whether the adjudicated delinquent can be placed on probation (which, incidentally, is better developed there than in most states) or otherwise left in the community for treatment, or requires placement in some type of institution.[5] In the latter event he is generally put under the direction of the Youth Authority. The processing begins with four to six weeks at a reception center, after which the treatment decision is made. On that basis the youngster may be released on parole or sent to a substitute home or to one of the many specialized treatment centers or camps, unless a mental institution is indicated. The Authority is also empowered to create places of detention, training-for-employment centers, and so forth, to the extent to which funds are available.

New Facilities for Adolescents

The upper age limit for juvenile court jurisdiction ranges from sixteen to eighteen and exceptionally up to twenty-one. It has tended to be raised as a result of official recommendations. In New York State, where the official juvenile must be under sixteen, some special provisions are made. Minors between sixteen and nineteen may be designated "youthful offenders" with the consent of the judge after investigation, provided the charge is not a crime punishable by death or life imprisonment. In that event they are treated somewhat along the lines of juvenile court procedure. The Wayward Minor Act made it possible to adjudicate as "wayward minors" adolescents between the ages of nineteen and twenty-one, for certain not too well-defined moral offenses, so that they could be placed on probation or committed to a reformatory for a period not exceeding three years. Several large cities maintain special courts for adolescents, in which procedures are geared to the objective of social rehabilitation.

The extension of certain juvenile court procedures to adolescents must be regarded as preferable to handling them in regular criminal court fashion. More effective recognition and treatment of adolescent problems would also result if special courts were more generally established for the hearing of adolescent cases, as is already done in three cities. The moral and social difficulties of adolescents are often of a different kind from those of juveniles. For this reason we regard the approach of the California Youth Authority as having special advantages. The Diagnostic Center at Menlo Park, New Jersey, and the Diagnostic Center at Madison, Wisconsin, are also well worthy of consideration.

A step in the same direction is the New York State Reception Center at Elmira. All convicted offenders between sixteen and twenty-one years of age are remanded to this center, which makes a careful investigation of the adolescent's problems, attitudes, and capabilities and on this basis decides to which of a considerable variety of institutions he should be sent. The Center is particularly concerned that the offender get whatever training he needs—not least, efficient and appropriate work training— and that every effort be made to find him a decent job when he leaves his institution.

The Family Court and Its Adjuncts

An insulated juvenile court has many limitations and defects. Often it cannot deal with the whole problem of the juvenile before it. Frequently, for example, there is neglect as well as delinquency. If neglect includes a parent's lack of support, that would probably go to a different court altogether. Or, if an issue of paternity arises, that again comes under the jurisdiction of a different court. Aside from such special situations, the problem of delinquency is a family problem in every sense.

The answer is the family court, dealing with domestic issues of all kinds. Cincinnati has had such a court for over thirty years; another good example is the Municipal Court of Philadelphia. New York State, after a long period of gestation over the integration of a highly segmented system of courts, has established a state-wide Family Court. Within this court the loose procedures of the former Children's Court have been tightened, with proper rules for admissible evidence and other safeguards to protect the legal rights of children. Among the provisions are a system of law guardians for children, easy methods for hearings to reconsider past orders or proceedings, and reasonably easy appeals from Family Court decisions.[6]

Moreover, the inclusive Family Court is in a stronger position for the interaction of the various services within its ambit. These services include the intake procedure, the adjustment bureau, the probation system, and the court clinic. Previously the connections among these were loose and ineffective. The intake process has often been poorly equipped and without sufficient status, unable to carry through an effective pre-investigation and screening procedure. The probation service has too often been poorly equipped, underpaid, lacking the qualifications its function called for. Good working relationships between the probation officer and the judge, or between the clinic staff and the probation officer, were often lacking. The clinic attached to the court was inadequately staffed, was slow in reporting back on cases, and was sometimes regarded by judges as failing to give them clear leads for a disposition. No doubt such defects might have been remedied to a degree within the limits of the juvenile court, but in the wider supervision and extended authority of the Family Court the opportunity is greater and the need more obvious. Under the leadership of Judge Florence Kelley, the Family Court has been developing in efficiency and range of service. At the same time there remains within the unified court system the tendency for its various sections—The Juvenile Term, the Family Offense Term, the Support and Conciliation Term, and so on—to act in a kind of quasi-independence.

An illustration of the potentialities of pre-investigation and screening was provided in an experiment under the auspices of the New York City Children's Court.[7] With the aid of a mental health team, a consultative process was set up, involving the probation department as well as the judge. During a six months' experimental period 1000 cases came under consideration. In a majority of these, the consultation sufficed to identify the nature of the problem investigated, for all concerned. Other cases called for more comprehensive diagnostic assessment. This service has been a source of great stimulation both to the intake department and the probation department.

The new probation service at intake has developed more recently in a very promising manner. Judge Justine Wise Polier testifies: "The achievement at intake in adjusting cases of children alleged to be delinquent or in need of supervision has already improved the whole picture in detention of children pending disposition. Among other contributing factors are the sharp drop in the number of delinquent children brought before the court on new petitions, the definite restrictions under the new law on the length of time the court may remand such children pending disposition, and the expansion of state facilities for children needing placement."

Judge Polier points out, however, that "for reasons that are not clear and require careful study, the new probation service at intake has been far more effective in cases where the child is alleged to be delinquent or in need of supervision than where a charge of neglect is lodged against parents. For the first six months of 1963, there was a decrease of 37 per cent in the number of children brought before the court on new delinquency and in-need-of-supervision petitions."[8]

In only a very few regions is any effort made to relate the

probation system to a diagnostic clinic. Another example is that of the Santa Clara County Juvenile Court, which has organized a psychiatric clinic to work with the probation service.[9] A main objective is to avert, through the union of the two services, the separate functioning that may well lead to further disorganization for an already disunited family.

Summation

Across the whole country much more needs to be done to make the juvenile court a fully efficient and cooperative agency within the network of services on behalf of youth. The court has a distinctive role. At a certain state in the delinquent's career the court has the crucial task of deciding whether he needs to become its ward and, if so, what form of treatment should follow. But it cannot properly perform this task unaided. The insulated self-sufficient juvenile court is an anachronism. The court itself has not the time or the experience to assess the complex problems of youth and their relation to the youth's family and environment. Both prior to and after court hearings, screening, consultative, and follow-up services are necessary if it is to fulfill the mission the community has entrusted to it. The following conditions we regard as primary.

1. Judges serving in juvenile courts should have special qualifications appropriate to their function. Some system should be adopted that would rule out patronage or other political ground for their selection. A list of candidates might, for example, be prepared by a bar association or other qualified body, the specific choice between them being made by the relevant municipal or state authority.

2. The intake system should be adequately equipped and qualified to investigate and screen out the cases that do not need to come before the court. In doing so, it should maintain close relations with the probation department and the diagnostic center where the latter exists. An effective intake service can relieve the judge of many needless hearings and enable him to concentrate more on those cases that require careful consideration.

3. The probation system, as the major and most promising of the resources available to the judge for disposition of cases, should be adequately staffed to permit the limiting of the caseload so that the probation officer has sufficient time and opportunity to give careful attention to the needs of every probationee, should be provided with a salary schedule adequate to attract fully qualified officers, and should be constituted as a professional service, with its own organization and a degree of autonomy.

4. Even where there is a superior probation service the judge can only exceptionally possess the requisite information and the expert comprehension of the adjudged delinquent's problems to determine the best mode of disposition. It is therefore highly desirable that the court have available a diagnostic center to which the more difficult cases would be referred for investigation and advisement. A psychiatric clinic does not suffice, since for many cases the skills of the clinical psychologist, the sociologist, the pediatrician, and the child welfare specialist are needed.

5. A promising type of over-all organization is a state youth authority to which adjudged delinquents would be committed for disposition. Such an authority should be empowered to utilize the available agencies, including educational and medical as well as correctional, and to create and develop needed facilities. It should have its own professionally staffed diagnostic center.

6. The socialized procedure of the juvenile court should be extended, so far as feasible, to adolescents up to the age of twenty-one.

7. Since the problem of delinquency is not detachable from a complex of problems concerning both the delinquent and his family, the juvenile court will operate with greater efficiency if it is integrated into the system of an inclusive family court.

15

The Custodial Institution

The number of children in New York State adjudicated delinquent and placed in public or private institutions increased from 1500 in 1949 to more than 3100 in 1962. However, in 39 counties of less than 100,000 population a substantial decrease (30 per cent) has occurred in the past five years. It would certainly be desirable to discover the reason for this disparity. In the larger cities the situation has been growing steadily worse.

While in 1949 less than half of the children committed in New York State went to state institutions, 80 per cent of those committed in 1962 went to state training institutions. In fact 95 per cent of the thirteen-year increase has been absorbed by these state-operated systems. Although voluntary institutions continue to play an important role in the development of services available to children in trouble, the major responsibility for institutional care now lies with the state training schools.[1]

Approximately 350 institutions in the United States serve children adjudicated delinquent. Of these one is a federal training school, 132 are state training schools (68 for boys, 50 for girls, 14 coeducational), 52 are county or city training schools, 11 are state reception diagnostic centers, 29 are forestry camps, and 135 are schools under private auspices. The public institutions accommodate approximately 36,000 delinquent children at any one time (and about 72,000 in the course of a year), while the private schools house approximately 10,000. The average age of the training school student nationally is close to 16 but the range is from under 10 to over 18 depending on state statute and policies. Seventy-five per cent are boys; two-thirds are white; 15 per cent have been in training schools before. Forty per cent of the institutions house over 200 children each (in fact, 15 institutions have capacities of 300 to 399 and 12 house over 400). More than half have capacities for more than 150 children. Many are overcrowded and are operating well beyond official capacity.[2] More than one-third of the training schools are housing more than the number of juveniles for whom they were designed.[3]

The custodial institution for juvenile offenders raises many questions. What is the rationale for commitment? How effective are the institutions as a means of rehabilitation? What should be done to improve their effectiveness? Into what different types do they fall? When are alternative methods of treatment preferable?

Types of Custodial Institutions

Custodial institutions may be broadly distinguished as those under public auspices, generally known as state training schools, and those under private auspices. Unlike institutions under private auspices, whether religious or philanthropic, the state institutions cannot pick and choose those inmates they regard as appropriate for their service. They are under obligation to admit, with few exceptions, the heterogeneous youngsters assigned to them. Both public and private institutions do a kind of internal selection, since both divide the inmates among a series of cottages, in which they spend the night under the charge of "cottage parents." The number in each cottage varies from an average of about twenty or less in the better-equipped institutions to an extreme of eighty. Some institutions under private auspices have led the way in the development of an all-round professional staff. On the average there is one full-time staff member (including educational and treatment officials, administrative, operational, and maintenance staff) for every 2.6 juveniles, but even so, as has been pointed out in some research studies, the staff members cannot cope adequately with the various needs of the diversity of youngsters under their charge.

The staffing of training schools has always been a problem. The quality of service that the care and treatment of difficult children demand is hard to recruit and harder to retain. Many of these schools are remote from urban areas, since they require considerable space and are not welcomed by the communities near which they might want to be located. While the more rural locations may have certain advantages, they create difficulties in securing the professional staff they need, especially as the conditions of life are arduous. Moreover, the salaries are often lower than are available elsewhere. Consequently the turnover is high, the median length of service for full-time staff employees being three years. Key staff vacancies often remain unfilled for considerable periods. Qualifications consequently have to be reduced to secure the necessary quota. This comment applies to teachers, psychologists, social workers, psychiatrists, and others, although some devoted staff members are of high quality. Few training schools have a full-time psychiatric service and some none at all. Perhaps the most difficult staffing problem for directors of training schools is finding "cottage parents." The juveniles spend more time under their charge than they do with any other members of the staff. The objective is to obtain the services of mature persons—preferably a husband and wife for each cottage—who understand the problems of children. But these desiderata are hard indeed to attain, and few are found who are really qualified for their difficult and exacting task.

Forestry schools and farm schools for delinquents may be considered varieties of state training schools. In some instances the differences are only secondary, since farming or market gardening is frequently an occupation for the youth in regular training schools, and forestry may have a relatively minor role

in schools designated as forestry. Forestry schools properly so
called probably have advantages for a select group of youngsters, but for the urban-bred population who constitute the great
bulk of adjudicated delinquents the evidence suggests that they
are by no means appropriate. Youngsters who have some feeling
for country life and work in the woods probably benefit and in
the forestry environment may feel less the chafing sense of custodial restraint. But further studies are needed to determine
the degree of success these institutions achieve.

There are certain differences between state institutions and
those under private auspices. In the first place the latter are
selective and put strict limits on their total intake. Thus they do
not reach the size of some of the very large state institutions.
The young under their care are somewhat more homogeneous,
so that treatment programs can be better concentrated. They
often refuse to accept highly disturbed delinquents, arsonists,
and others who show dangerous tendencies. They tend to have a
larger proportion of professional workers. We may distinguish
those under religious auspices, since they tend to select youth
whose families belong to the faith the institutions represent and
they lay more stress on religious training. Many of these institutions are under Roman Catholic auspices, with a few under
Jewish auspices. The private institutions not under the auspices
of a particular religion tend to be somewhat more experimental
in their modes of treatment. Those we have personally studied
in the New York area, going under the name of "residential
treatment centers," have shown considerable readiness to try
out various approaches to meet their insistent problems.[4] Institutions such as Wiltwyck and Children's Village—and also
Hawthorne–Cedar Knolls, which is under Jewish auspices—
proved to be excellent examples of their kind. If their success
is still quite limited we find in this fact some corroboration of
our contention that custodial institutions should be resorted to
only when it is imperative, to protect the public and the child
himself, to place the youth under custodial care.

We leave for later consideration certain smaller and more
specialized residential centers as well as the "halfway houses"

usually located in cities as temporary supervisory abodes particularly for youths discharged from the larger institutions.

The Basis of Institutional Commitment

Now we turn to our critical questions. First, how are commitments to institutions made and on what grounds? When a youngster is adjudged delinquent by a court, the main alternatives at the disposal of the judge are to put him on probation or to send him to an institution. It is presumed that those committed are the "hard core" of delinquent children who have been in trouble several times and have failed to respond to warnings and to neighborly services. The majority have been on probation previously without showing any improvement. We have, however, pointed out that probation services often provide only nominal or quite perfunctory supervision and are of little or no benefit to the probationees. Some are committed who have no previous records but have been arrested for felonies of a type that cause serious concern. Some are committed, however, because their delinquency is associated with bad home conditions, and the judge feels that, for lack of better alternatives, it is desirable to remove them from home and place them under custodial care.

We may regard the preceding statements as the rationale of judicial commitment. But actually when we examine cases with any care we find no clear line of principle underlying the most serious decision the judge has to make—that is, to commit a youngster to an institution. Joseph H. Louchheim concludes from his study of commitments that the decision is based on expediency rather than on social planning.[5] In our own study of the commitment practices in New York City we found strong evidence indicating that the decision to commit to an institution is often made without adequate consideration of the nature of the case. As Louchheim states, a large number of young people are committed after their first court appearance, and a very considerable number without their having had contact with community resources.

Increasing commitments and pressures from the courts have led to the creation of additional public institutions. At least part of the reason, as Alfred J. Kahn points out in a study conducted for the New York State Department of Welfare, is that the judges could find no more appropriate recourse available. New York and some other states are now making efforts to provide such alternatives as halfway houses, foster homes, and urban group residences.

Were adequate alternatives available, it would be sound strategy on the part of the juvenile courts to limit to the absolute minimum (a consideration we shall presently explore) the number of cases committed to large institutions such as our present state training schools.

We should distinguish here between two types of alternatives. One is a variety of small residence, with a more homelike attitude, specialized for the different needs and problems of the young. Children who suffer mainly from neglect should not be mixed with children who have confirmed delinquent habits. Children suffering from physical handicaps or ailments should be treated in some form of hospital or hospital department where they can receive the treatment they need. Children who exhibit particularly dangerous tendencies—arsonists, nonstatutory rapists, sadistically violent children—should be segregated from other delinquents and given particular care under qualified experts, as should children who exhibit psychotic or other mental disturbances. We must always remember that the function of children's courts is not to punish, that they are not criminal courts, but are expressly set up to assure that children will receive the care, treatment, or therapy their particular problems demand.

The other type of alternative consists of directive and protective supervision, as well as therapeutic treatment, which does not require the removal of the youth from his own home environment. The most important resort of this kind is probation, which, with an adequate staff of really qualified probation officers, could be most advantageously employed for many cases that are now committed to institutions.

The Case Against Institutionalization

The reasons we believe that institutionalization should be avoided whenever possible are particularly relevant to large-scale institutions such as the great majority of our present state training schools, but they also apply, to some degree, to all types of institutions that remove children from the home environment.

In the first place, the institutional setting is for the young delinquent an alien one that militates against his responsiveness to even the best and wisest treatment. Technically, the institution is a place where the youth is sent for friendly guidance and training, but for the youth himself it is a prison, a punishment. He is cut off from all familiar associations. He is under restraints that he bitterly resents. He lives with other youths who are equally resentful, and his only friends are those who inspire him with hostility to the authorities who have him in their charge. His relationships fall within the range of a one-sex, one-age society, among the disadvantages of which is its effect on the sexual attitude of the inmates. We must remember that these youths have, perhaps more than others of their age, associated with "girl friends" in their home environment. There is considerable evidence that the system encourages homosexuality. This is as true of the institutions for girls as of those for boys.[6]

The second count is directly associated with the first. It is the simplest principle of social behavior that likes gang up with their likes against unlikes. So do the rebellious inmates of these institutions, just as do the inmates of prisons. But for these youthful delinquents the effects are more serious. The staff is seeking to instill socialized attitudes. To frustrate the intentions of the staff, to evade the rules, at most to comply with tongue in cheek, is the natural response of the inmates. The tougher boys dominate the others. They bully the weaker and any who are minded to comply with institutional requirements. We have some evidence that entering boys are more amenable and sometimes more desirous of making a good adjustment within the institution than the same boys after they have been initiated into the mores of the institutional "subculture." Some institutional administrators tend to accommodate themselves into a kind of acquiescence with these mores within the limits that permit a degree of "coexistence."[7] One investigator, Seymour Rubenfeld, asserts that a fuller recognition of the character of the inmate society could open up a new dimension in the development of rehabilitation techniques.[8] A fuller recognition of the needs and conditions that are responsible for inmate resort to underground resistance would probably avoid mistakes and frustrations on the part of the staff, but how much more it could achieve is debatable. The youthful underground is analogous to the kind of street gang to which so many of its members have belonged and carries on the gang's characteristics so far as institutional conditions permit. In the institution, where there are no distracting outside influences on gang members, ruthless control is all the more assured.

Howard W. Polsky's study, *Cottage Six,* offers a realistic appraisal of the operation of the inmate subculture inside a first-rate residential treatment institution.[9] He points out that every boy found it necessary to adopt the values and patterns of the subculture, regardless of the system of treatment including clinical therapy. Not only was the subculture the dominant force in the life of the boys but it was potent enough to evoke a kind of covert and unwitting support from the staff itself. The removal of "key" boys did not appear to modify its effectiveness in the least. The subculture has its own social system which stabilizes and unifies its pathways. Polsky's findings have led the institution in question to make the cottage as a whole and not the individual boy the basic unit of treatment, taking into account the nature of the experience the boys collectively share. How effective this recent change of approach will be remains to be seen.

The third reason for our viewpoint is the evidence of recidivism. Various studies of children's courts, as Bloch and Flynn point out, indicate that as high as 60 to 80 per cent of the inmates of state training schools fail to make good within five years or more after discharge.[10] Mannering reported that 41 per cent of those discharged from the Wisconsin School for Boys failed within the year and 50 per cent within two years.[11] We have a variety of other figures for various institutions, but we do not cite them because they cover relatively short periods or depend on an inadequate sampling. The fact is that there has been very little serious research into the extent of recidivism. Considerable expense is involved and thorough research covering a period of years is necessary. Many of those who have been in institutions disappear from view, and it is hard to find those who have moved to another address or left their home city. One reasonably good indication, however, is the number of parolees from institutions who were recommitted. For parolees under the supervision of the California Youth Authority the figure cited over a number of years is around 45 per cent, while an additional 24 per cent were discharged from parole "under suspension," usually because the responsibility for the youth was transferred to another agency. We cannot assume that the parolees who are not convicted of further offenses can therefore be regarded as "successes," since it is a well-recognized fact that a considerable number of law violations are either not reported at all or the perpetrators are not discovered. On the other hand, there are a few instances in which the rate of recidivism reported is much lower. Thus Berkshire Farms Training School in New York State reported a "success rate" of 75 per cent for boys over 15½ years and 53 per cent for those under 15½ years.[12] Part of the explanation in this instance may be the fact that this school had an excellent official who was particularly helpful in caring for and finding employment for the boys discharged from the institution.

Our conclusion agrees with that of other investigators including Jerome Laulicht and Herbert Bloch, that the results of training school experiences are discouraging. Nor can we attribute this situation to the inefficiency of the institutions themselves. Not only do they work under considerable handicaps but many of their inmates are the most serious and confirmed delinquents with whom the courts have to deal. The fact that so many of them come up for adjudication without having previously received any proper care or treatment constitutes a strong indictment against a system that gives relatively little attention to the need for early care and guidance for vulnerable children and those beginning to exhibit delinquent tendencies.

There is another important reason why our custodial institutions so often fail in their mission of rehabilitation, and that is the inadequacy of after-care. The transition from the guarded, relatively regimented, remote and alien life of the institution to the youth's own neighborhood, with its new freedom and its associations good or bad, is a crucial experience. The parolee is suddenly faced with difficult problems. Whether he goes back to school or is old enough to seek employment, he has a count against him. He is under suspicion, a marked youth. His old gang welcomes him back. The line of least resistance, together with his burning desire to exert his regained freedom, leads him back to his old haunts and his old ways. If, as often enough happens, he cannot find a job, what is left for him but to drift into a criminal career? This is the time when above all he needs assurance, friendly protection, and aid in making a living. But often enough he is dumped out of the institution bus to find his own road with only the most casual supervision. The U.S. Senate Delinquency Subcommittee reported in 1958 that after-care was one of the most vulnerable aspects of the entire anti-delinquency effort.

One condition that has retarded the provision of after-care is the lack of any clear decision as to whose responsibility it is. Actually the institutions themselves have been most active in seeking to secure it, but their resources are usually quite inadequate for this additional service. Some of it has been supplied through State, local, and private welfare agencies. But very much remains to be done, and in many states mighty little is done in comparison with the need. The new youth employment policies, combined with the whole antipoverty program of the Federal Government, give promise of meeting an important part of this need. Nothing is more essential for the youth who is discharged from an institution than to be assured of a decent job, or, if he is not yet ready for one, to be provided under good auspices with the training that will qualify him for one. The institutions themselves are recognizing the need to train their inmates realistically for their working life, but usually they cannot do much more than initiate the work-training process. In other ways also the superior institutions do all they can to facilitate the transition from the more cloistered life to that of the youth's neighborhood. Children's Village, for example, has a terminal period during which every aspect of the returnee's relationship with the neighborhood is explored, including school recognition, job placement, family acceptability and alternatives where necessary, membership in a community center, church affiliation, if any, and so forth.[13] For the same purpose, the State of California has set up a liaison procedural plan to provide, after the youth leaves, an individualized social service, employment opportunities, family assistance and guidance, and general supervision.[14] North Carolina also, on a statewide basis, has made plans for after-care, with various types of aid through the transition period.[15]

A final reason why some alternative to institutionalization should be preferred wherever feasible is that the alternatives are considerably less costly. The annual maintenance cost per inmate in our major custodial institutions runs from $3500 to around $7500. There is, besides, the large capital outlay required for the extensive grounds and numerous buildings such institutions require. A tenth of the total annual cost of one such institution could pay for great and much needed developments in the probation services of the community.

Some New Types of Institutions

Custodial institutions will always be necessary. There are youths who must, because they are too dangerous, too uncontrolled, too vicious to be at large, be segregated for a period from their society while they are young enough to admit the hope that under training they may still be rehabilitated. It is therefore highly important that this difficult service be under the charge of the most qualified as well as the most devoted staff that can be procured, and that the programs themselves be as appropriate and efficient as expert research can devise. Our best institutions now experiment with "milieu" therapy, group therapy, art therapy, and as much clinical treatment as they are able to provide, following the lead of such residential treatment centers as Wiltwyck and Hawthorne–Cedar Knolls, but they can give intensive treatment to only a small proportion of the inmate population, which is constantly changing.

Besides such institutions there are a few that break new ground and point up some developments which may be of moment for the future. One type is represented by the Highfields Group Center in New Jersey; another is known as the "Provo experiment." Both types offer substitutes for the large walled all-containing custodial systems.[16]

Highfields is a compact institution containing about twenty boys at any one time. It has these special features: employment of the boys away from the institution, thus enabling them to have regular contacts with the outside world, followed by group inter-action sessions in the evening. The work supervisor takes the boys each morning to some relatively near-by state hospital, where they are assigned specific jobs under the direction of hos-pital employees and the oversight of the work supervisor. They work in the storehouse, the garage, the butcher shop, the linen room, the farm, or wherever they may be needed. The work supervisor is concerned with the problems the boys may exhibit in their working habits and job relationships.

Of considerable significance are the group interaction get-togethers, a kind of "bull session" but under unobtrusive direc-tive guidance, an initiation to a process of social accommodation, testing out the attitudes of the inmates and exploring their de-fensive or hostile reactions. As the sessions proceed the boys are posed with alternatives between which they are to decide, be-tween the old way of life and a new way. The boys are at cross purposes, some more responsive, some resistant. Cliques are formed. The attainment of some form of group solidarity is at issue. Many of the youths become clearly aware that if they are to find a place in free society, they must change their attitudes and their modes of behavior.

In the final stage there is some probing of the problems of individual members, the therapist confining himself to a minimum of guidance. The members review their interrelations at Highfields and their home-ground relationships, their own past and present behavior. The whole process is free from formality. It is geared to evoking in the youth himself a new awareness of his own behavior as he learns to see it through the eyes of others and discovers that there are better ways to cope with his own problems.

The preceding is a very sketchy summary of the Highfields approach. There is nothing authoritarian about it. Its rules are simple, and they are enforced through the imposition of extra duties on the violators, though boys who are wholly unamenable are returned to court for an alternative and more forbidding disposition. The length of stay is normally about four months— much less than the average elsewhere. The combination of steady daily work of a normal kind outside the institution combines with the evocative evening sessions, in which each member of a relatively small group is given full freedom to find a way to express himself in his relation to others, to create a favorable atmosphere wholly unlike any these youth have known before.

The test of recidivism is pretty well met, and Highfields, unlike some institutions, has endeavored to test in this way the results of its work. A comparison in this respect made between Highfields and the state reformatory at Annandale shows that recidivism rates of Highfield boys were substantially lower and their rates of adjustment to social life considerably higher for one year to five years after discharge.[17] We must, however, remember that Highfields received a relatively selected group, those whom the court regarded as cases appropriate for this institution. But when comparable samples from the two institutions were taken, Highfields still had a very much better showing.

Highfields has certainly challenged some of the assumptions on which most custodial institutions for youths are conducted. Is there any advantage, and is there not some disadvantage, in retaining boys or girls for periods ranging from eight months to two and sometimes even three years—aside, that is, from quite special cases? Highfields appears to do better within a period of three to four months. Highfields is so run that it needs a considerably smaller staff in relation to the number of inmates than do most institutions, and for that and other reasons operates at a considerably lower per capita cost. It is a small-scale institution; its rules are simple and relatively few; it has no formal orientation period, no elaborate testing; it offers the boys a full working day outside of the institution, in contact with ordinary working people. All these differences, in addition to its special type of group therapy, raise significant questions regarding the whole process of institutionalization.

Our second exhibit is the Provo experiment with its focus at Pinehills, Utah.[18] It was organized and is directed under the auspices of the juvenile court, as proposed by an advisory council of laymen and professionals. Its officials are deputy probation officers appointed by the court. It is planned for habitual offenders, fifteen to seventeen years old, excluding psychotics and highly disturbed youth. In a number of respects it resembles the Highfields plan. There is no formal structure, no testing, no clinical diagnosis. The weight of important decisions is placed on the youth themselves. The group is small, no more than twenty being permitted at any one time. The key principle is that of group interaction. A regular job is prescribed, and if a boy has already a full-time job he is allowed to continue at it. The stay at the institution is not very different from that at Highfields, being usually from four to seven months. But one important difference is that the youngsters remain at home and are taken by automobile to Pinehills.

The first objective is to weld the group into a coherent whole. It is up to the group to develop a system of attitudes and mores that directs its members away from the delinquent habits of the outside groups they had associated with. The pressure on them is intended to involve them in their new group and to have it set up its own set of antidelinquent mores. The youths are free to devise situations in which they have to make their own decisions. If a boy refuses to become involved he comes under attack from the boys who are. Moreover, he knows that if he is recalcitrant he becomes a candidate for a reformatory. All the boys know that their release depends on their exhibiting a sense of involvement. It is, however, more the behavior of the youth when outside the group—a matter on which information is generally available—than his behavior within it that is made the test of his acceptance of the group-spirit and of his readiness for release.

The boys are thus taught to look to themselves for a way out of their problems. The authorities do not try to be pals with the boys. They are instigators of a group process, not regular participants in it. They do, however, apply various sanctions against any boy who fails in due time to engage in the process, ranging from docking his pay to sending him to prison for a week-end, and in the last resort to returning him to court for another and less agreeable disposition. The emphasis is put on the rejection of delinquent values through group interaction and on the establishment of good work habits. The newer boys are prompted by the older ones. The finding of employment for the boys is a permanent task of the authorities.

A careful effort is made to evaluate the results of this treatment, intended to cover a period of five years. Two types of control groups provide a basis for assessment, one a similar group of offenders who are placed on probation and the other a comparable group who are sent to the Utah Industrial School. The conclusions of this comparative study were not yet available at the time of writing.

Finally, we should note that the cost per youth under the Provo system is about one-tenth what it would have been had he been sent to a regular reformatory.

Group Residence Programs

We have spoken of the imperative need for after-care in the difficult transition period experienced by youth on their discharge from institutions. It remains to take account of a device that has an institutional aspect but at the same time is intended

as a means of transition to the ordinary life of the community—
a device frequently described as a "halfway house." For many
returnees the group residence is an excellent solution of the problem of transition. It allows them the freedom of a social life
within and outside the residence. They are looked after and
have their immediate needs met. They have counselors and ad-
visers, but they are no longer under guard or subject to an
authority who tells them what to do. Some residences provide
job training or opportunities to secure it, as well as help in job
placement, a highly important consideration. These residences
are eminently suitable for those who cannot without peril be returned to a bad home or directly to their old environment, and
some youths need the associations and the moral support of this
kind of residential club to make good as parolees. We have in
mind one case: a boy who had a poor and broken home life,
drifted into delinquency, and after a time in a training school
was paroled to a foster home with no success. Two other foster
home placements were equally unsuccessful. But when he was
tried out in a group residence in Manhattan he responded well
and has ever since continued to make good. Now married and
continuing in his original employment he is attending college
classes in the evening.

A much greater development of these group residences is
needed. For many thousands of young persons being returned to
our cities every year such residences might make all the difference between downfall and a new more hopeful existence.[19] A
considerable expenditure is required, but the cost per annum is
still only about half that of the institutional training they have
received, and might often make the difference between a wasted
expenditure for the stay in the institution and a real social gain.
The results of group residence appear to be good in a fairly high
percentage of cases, though further investigation is desirable.
The British probation hostels, in which the probationer volun-
tarily agrees to remain for a year, have won favor as being
suitable for properly selected youngsters. Several states, including Wisconsin, New York, and Ohio, have already developed a
number of such residences and contributed useful information

on the conditions and the modes of operation that prove most expedient. Municipalities, welfare agencies, training schools, and residential treatment centers have also set up a small number of such residences.

The Planning of Institutional Facilities

It is of high importance that our authorities break away from the uniformity of large-scale unspecialized institutions for delinquent youth. The case is already clear for the advantage of small-scale compact institutions housing twenty or thirty young persons where they can establish closer relations with a small staff, and where the danger of a rebel underground is minimized. Such small institutions make specialization possible; children who suffer from neglect more than from a confirmed habit of delinquency need no longer be housed with those who have a thoroughly bad record. We have considerable evidence from state training schools that these schools are compelled to accept children suffering from physical handicaps, specific health problems, or mental ailments that call for specialized treatment which they cannot provide. We have been informed by a competent authority in a hospital for psychotics that disturbed young persons who should not be so classified are admitted there. Intake records designate many varieties of problem children under the broad categories "disturbed," "highly disturbed," "mentally disturbed," and often no more authoritative classification is made before commitment. All such misplacements, which may have very serious consequences, could be avoided with a properly differentiated system of small-scale institutions.

To secure that end it is essential, on the one hand, that each state have an expert body, or a special committee of the over-all authority responsible for state institutions for delinquents, to plan and put into effect the setting up and organization of these institutions, and, on the other hand, a diagnostic clinic under a Youth Authority or attached to the relevant courts with the function of assigning cases to appropriate institutions in all instances where the judge decides that institutional commitment is re-

quired. Should such a body conclude that some alternative to institutional treatment is preferable, it would advise the court to that effect.

Summation and Recommendations

The present institutional system for the treatment of adjudged delinquents raises many questions and is the subject of considerable controversy. What types of juveniles need the drastic remedy of institutional treatment? What types of institutions are proper for different forms of delinquent behavior? How should the length of stay be determined? No ready answers are available, aside from the fact that we have as yet no great variety of institutional types. Here, as elsewhere, conclusions are handicapped by the fact that far more has been done to provide reasonably good if still inadequate institutions than to develop the alternative modes of disposition, and particularly the major alternative of probation. Until the function and the potentialities of probation are better realized and fulfilled no meaningful study of the respective success or failure of the two alternatives will be possible.

It is generally agreed that when there is a manifest hazard either to the community or to the juvenile in leaving him in his home environment, some form of institutionalization is desirable. But relatively little has been done to differentiate institutions so that the various categories of young delinquents are respectively provided with the kind of institution and of therapy best suited to their needs.

Our conclusions respecting strategy may be summed up as follows:

1. In view of the handicaps of institutional living, it should not be imposed where there is a reasonable chance that probation or other treatment that does not remove the juvenile from his home environment can be effective.

2. The hazard of institutionalization can be reduced by the establishment of small-scale institutions admitting closer and more informal relations between inmates and staff. Such institutions have also the very great merit that they can be

specialized for the different needs of the various categories of problem children.

3. Neglected or homeless juveniles, especially the younger ones, unless their offenses are particularly serious, should not be sent to training schools or similar institutions, but to householdlike shelters or foster homes. Juveniles suffering from physical handicaps or mental troubles should be assigned to special treatment centers equipped for the therapy they need.

4. Much experimentation is desirable in planning diversified institutions and also in determining the length of residence and the conditions of release. Such planning should be conducted through a specially qualified arm of the state or other authority responsible for the control and prevention of delinquency.

5. The period of transition from the institution to the community is a particularly important one, in which the returnee needs neighborly counsel, help in forming new associations, job training and employment opportunities. Without such after-care any benefit he may have received from institutional treatment may be wholly dissipated. For some parolees group residences or "halfway houses" are very serviceable. The whole matter of after-care calls for much fuller examination and provision than it has generally received.

Treatment Systems

While any service for the control or prevention of delinquency might be broadly called "treatment," the term is more specifically applicable to concerted programs under professional guidance. Recently a considerable number of such programs have been developed, with varying emphases and approaches. Of those the most promising recognize the complexity of the conditions directly associated with delinquency and endeavor to deal with the various aspects of the problem, considering the whole background of the youth under observation—not only their attitudes but also their family situation, their health, their associations, and so forth.

The datum is a delinquency habit, sufficiently confirmed to require remedial or preventive intervention. This habit has its particular history in each case; that history needs to be studied, and to do so effectively rapport must be established with the youth and as far as possible with his family. The task is one that calls for much patience and skillful probing on the part of the professional staff.

In carrying out such a program the workers tend to classify the youths under treatment into different categories. The formulation of such typologies is a significant and characteristic feature of recent researches and, usually in a looser way, of the procedures of the treatment staff. Usually the categories are defined along psychological or psychoanalytic lines. Although clear demarcations between the projected types seem impossible to make, they may still give useful leads for treatment purposes. There is not and does not appear likely to be any authoritative classification. Moreover, it is risky to use the classifications for purposes of prediction. A good warning is provided by an eight-year follow-up of a school population rated at the age of fourteen by use of the Minnesota Multiphasic Personality Inventory.[1] Seventy-one cases coded as nondelinquent which turned out delinquent were characterized generally as coming from the most seriously disturbed homes. Also included in the follow-up test were seventy-one cases coded as delinquent which actually were found nondelinquent. These were compared on the one hand with an equal number of cases in which the prediction of delinquency proved to be accurate and a similar number coded as nondelinquent who remained so. The third group was presumed to be wedded to a delinquent subculture. Whatever the categories used, the predictive test is obviously an unsafe ground on which to select for treatment. An incidental finding deserves notice— of recorded delinquents at the age of nineteen only 22 per cent were found to have committed further delinquency by the age of twenty-three.

Two Primary Considerations

This follow-up test, one of the few thoroughgoing ones we have, confirms a conclusion on which we have already insisted. It is of primary importance that all vulnerable young people be detected at the earliest possible stage and given special care, guidance, protection, and, if need be, therapy. Under "vulnerables" we include not only children who have shown incipient delinquent tendencies but also those who are subjected to unhappy family situations or who are forming associations that may lead them into delinquency. Wherever there is disturbance or instability in the young, early remedial aid, under wisely sympathetic direction, can be vital for future well-being. But for the most part this lesson has still to be learned.

While specific typologies remain problematic, some simple correlations are clearly established. In the first place, the intrafamily experience of the youth is crucial. The association between delinquency and the neglect, indifference, or harsh or arbitrary attitude of parents, the lack of reasonable discipline or the pampering of a child's every whim, is of paramount importance. Where the home offers no social anchorage for the child, he becomes disoriented, disturbed, adrift. He manifests it by being withdrawn and sullen, or aggressive with a tendency to seek satisfaction in illicit ways. He becomes susceptible to dangerous promptings. For a child thus rendered vulnerable, the pressures of poverty, accidents, or misfortunes, or other untoward circumstances, or the association with other rebellious youth can easily turn the scale to the formation of delinquent ways.

This conclusion is wholly or partly supported by many studies of the subject, including those by the McCords, Wattenberg, Wolberg, Slocum and Stone, and the New York City Youth Board.[2] A recent English study presented significant evidence to the effect that in poor neighborhoods the determination of delinquency is home-centered, not neighborhood-centered. The bad neighborhood triggers the susceptibility created by experiences in the family.[3]

If we accept this conclusion it by no means implies that the adverse environment of the slum is not a significant factor in the causation of delinquency. The pressures of poverty within— fraying tempers and the stultifying of simple desires—are reinforced by the meanness and squalor without, which in turn offer no decent outlets for youthful energies. The high delinquency rates of such areas are a measure of the extent to which susceptibility to transgression, usually engendered within the family, is confirmed by life under slum conditions.

The initiating significance of the family is suggested by another finding from the English study mentioned above. This gave evidence that families living in relative isolation in low-delinquency areas exhibited the delinquency rates characteristic of high-delinquency areas. The interpretation of this finding calls for further study, and it would be important to discover how far it is corroborated by other researchers, but the assumption is tenable that when a family lives in near-isolation from its neighbors it has peculiar characteristics or special problems that may well lead the children to break away in revulsion or rebelliousness.

A second important consideration is that anything that interferes with or interrupts the process of child development can induce a train of consequences that may lead to delinquent ways. Such an event may happen in the nursery, in the playground, in the school, on the street, as well as in the home. To the sensitive child any accident may be traumatic. It may be a change of residence, where the child cannot adapt to the new conditions. The school is not infrequently the starting point of a series of troubles, occasioned by the inability to get along with a teacher, the failure to make the grade, perhaps evoking angry reproaches from a parent who fails to understand the child's problem, or the bullying of a bigger boy. With older youth the break may come because a parent insists that the son prepare to enter his father's business whereas the youth is determined to become something else, say an artist or a scientist. There are also situations in which the driving ambitions of a father or mother spur the child to try to achieve beyond his capacity or his energy, bringing tensions that lead to rebelliousness.

The two major considerations we have dwelt on could well be the premises on which a treatment system is based. They suggest the importance of acquiring an understanding of the history of the youth under treatment. The investigator must be able to put himself in the position of the young, to see the world with their perspectives.

This is not easy. It demands much skill and patience and devotion on the part of the investigators. To restore the disturbed balance or establish a new one requires the felicity of the artist as well as the competence of the trained worker. Across the country numerous programs of treatment are now in operation. We have a record of 143 communities in which programs for problem-beset families have been set up.[4] Some of them are still in the planning stage. Some of them employ the traditional casework approach. Some focus treatment on limited objectives, such as teaching homemaking skills or budgeting efficiency. It is a promising movement, but it remains questionable whether many of these programs are thoroughgoing enough to come to grips with the complexity of the problem. Few of these projects employ clearly defined measurement scales. Still fewer use control groups or have any adequate plans for a follow-up accounting.

Some Ground-Breaking Treatment Systems

We shall accordingly confine our review to certain well-directed and well-organized programs. One of these is the Hyde Park Youth Project in Chicago, an attempt to provide and test a coordinated approach to the treatment and prevention of serious youth troubles.[5] The neighborhood in which it is based is one in which the majority of families are above the poverty level, so that the problems to be met are directly intrafamilial or interpersonal. Of the 266 families involved, half the referrals came from the school, one-fifth from the police, and a small number through the Hyde Park Neighborhood Club. The problem of "reaching" the families for the initial diagnostic and treatment-planning stage appears to have been successfully met in a large proportion of the cases, and only a small percentage of the cases thus reached withdrew from the program prescribed. To supply whatever help seemed needed the available resources of the community were scouted and mustered. The planning appears to have been supervised with care, and the ratings recorded a not inconsiderable degree of success, with 15 per cent rated as showing "substantial improvement" and 38 per cent "some improvement."

An interesting development has been proceeding at the Wiltwyck School for Boys, one of the residential treatment centers that accepts boys committed from the New York City Domestic Relations Court.[6] The form of treatment is family therapy. (The same principle—that the problem of the youth is intimately related to and may be dependent upon the problem of the parents—is also appreciated by other treatment systems, for example the California Community Treatment Project.) It is recognized that the alienation of young people from their families, the absence of trust, the sense of having no haven is a deprivation that may bite deeply into morale. In earlier clinical work at Wiltwyck it was found that a large percentage of the parents of these boys had abdicated or were unqualified to perform the task of bringing up their children. A frequent result was that the family siblings became a subgroup on their own, following their own devices and the rough manners of the street. To restore some sense of family cohesion and to re-establish some intrafamily responsibility were the major aims of the program, and it has been undertaken with much discretion and careful and patient planning. To assist in the process the fullest aid, financial and other, was sought from the available public services. Practical approaches have been utilized to stimulate a focus of leadership within the family, to instruct in the management of the family budget, and to prepare and train the teenagers for the role of being a support to the household.

A particularly promising experiment in treatment has been inaugurated under the auspices of the California Youth Authority.[7] It is designed to study the feasibility of substituting an intensive community program for the traditional state training school system. It takes selected Youth Authority wards directly from a reception center to a community treatment center. This program, which already shows promise, could be of signal importance as supplying a preferable alternative to the risky and costly expedient of training-school custody.

The program is designed to provide different treatment for various defined types of delinquents. To enable the case work to be effective and sufficiently intensive, the average worker is given only eight cases. The communities involved were reluctant in the beginning to reaccept trouble-making youth who had recently been taken out of them for the good of all concerned and thereafter to participate in the rehabilitation process. But through a good public relations policy and the offer of special inducements the difficulty was largely overcome.

Diagnostic preparation is followed by a wide range of services, with counseling, tutoring, and group therapy adapted to diagnostic indications. Very considerable use is made of foster homes, and there are discussion groups for foster parents as well as for natural parents. Special efforts have been made to control the behavior of wards returned to the schools, since half of all the cases had given disciplinary trouble there.

The history of one such case may be cited briefly to show that wise coaching backed by the necessary discipline can sometimes succeed.[8] Tommy, aged thirteen, when committed to the Youth Authority, was being considered for permament exclusion from school, where he had frequently been defiant, malicious, and quarrelsome. After various conferences with school authorities he was given "one more chance." The understanding was that any infraction whatever would immediately send him to detention. Tommy tested the situation right at the start by "sassing" a teacher, forthwith followed by a week's detention. Tommy was so weak in internal controls that this resort was considered the appropriate one for his type. During the next six months only two rule infractions occurred, each immediately followed by a return to detention. The school authorities were much impressed not only by the vigilance of the authority's agency but also by the improvement in Tommy's behavior. The story, so far as we now have it, ends with the statement that Tommy is still frequently called into the school office but mostly now for commendation.

One conclusion which the Youth Authority's committee reached may have an important bearing on the crucial question of how far intra-community treatment is feasible and preferable as an alternative to custodial institutionalization. The conclusion was that not a single case in the experimental group was unsuitable for treatment in the community. Some of the wards who looked like being the worst cases (mainly very low-maturity youths) proved to be more amenable to the treatment than some of those rated as high maturity cases.[9] The infantile, querulous, complaining type proved remarkably susceptible to a system which provided strong controls over behavior combined with comfort, good food, and continuous patient tolerance of fumbling and abusiveness. Nearly all in this category required placement in carefully selected foster homes and almost daily contact with the community agent. The degree of success achieved with such cases and the unexpected emotional growth some of them exhibited were beyond the staff's expectations; in fact there was an impression that some of the 25 per cent regarded as ineligible could have been treated successfully under the program.

Most of those under treatment for six months or more showed a decrease in the frequency of misbehavior, and even more of those in the program for more than a year. The experimental cases had an average of forty-seven months per failure in the community while the control group averaged twenty-six months per failure.

The committee in charge divided the cases into three major categories—low maturity, middle maturity, and high maturity— but it also defined a series of delinquency subtypes and became convinced that this classification held good for differential treatment. The responsiveness to treatment varied with all nine subtypes, but the numbers under consideration in each were too small to make the statistical evidence very significant. The distinctions between subtypes, while competently formulated, raise some interesting problems that are too complex to be examined here. The staff, it should be noted, was enthusiastic about the contribution to successful treatment made by the differentiation into subtypes.

We regard this experiment under the California Youth Authority, a body which has been otherwise forward in antidelinquency programs, as the most promising lead in the strategy of rehabilitative treatment. It is one that might well be studied and followed by other states.

The Treatment of Drug Addiction

There are some special behavior problems that call for entirely distinctive modes of treatment. It is a significant age-old fact that when a form of behavior is offensive to the prevalent moral code the treatment has been almost universally to punish the offender, to resort to forcible suppression. This has been true for alcoholics, narcotics addicts, prostitutes, and homosexuals. A famous legislator of ancient Greece prescribed a double penalty for those who committed misdeeds under the influence of alcohol, first the penalty for the misdeed and second the penalty for being drunk. Only in very recent times has there been any recognition that mere punishment does not cure and may well aggravate the trouble, and that the only hope lies in skilled research into methods of treatment that can restore the "patient" or at least alleviate the condition so that he has a chance to live a more normal life again among his fellow men.

We shall consider here the question of treatment for only one of the problems mentioned—that of narcotics addiction, which rather recently has taken on an alarming association with juvenile delinquency. It is a practice that is fraught with a peculiar danger for those who yield to it. There are numbers of young delinquents who grow out of their rebelliousness and wildness as they find a steady job, become sufficiently interested in a girl to want a permanent attachment, and thus recognize the necessity of earning a decent living. There are others who, when caught young enough, benefit from well-designed treatment and reform. But the drug addict is caught in the vise of his habit and without the most careful treatment cannot break it off. He is its prisoner throughout a life of degradation and wretchedness.

The drug addict becomes much less inclined to go rioting around or commit wanton offenses. His offenses are mainly the consequence of his addiction, of his desperate need to obtain by any possible means the funds that will enable him to satisfy his daily craving. This may account for the decline in gang wars in recent years, especially in areas where there is considerable evidence of the resort to narcotic drugs. The slave of the habit ceases to be gregarious.

There are two ways in which young people are drawn into this snare. One is as a drastic form of escapism, a respite from the burden of failure and deprivation and the bleakness of an opportunityless future. It is significant that drug addiction is more commonly found among poverty-stricken youth who are also discriminated against, Puerto Ricans and Negroes, for example. The other way is for "kicks." Here the use of drugs is likely to begin at juvenile parties where marijuana cigarettes are smoked. If that habit takes hold, the next step is to graduate to heroin or an equivalent, and the trap begins to close. Recent reports show that drug addiction has made inroads in several relatively prosperous areas. Addition can become, as a federal narcotic agent put it, "an infectious disease."

The treatment of narcotic addicts, adult or juvenile, has been so far mostly an unhappy affair. Addicts have been consigned to hospital wards, special hospitals, detention houses, or prisons—arrests usually are made when, as is so frequently the case, the addict has been charged with theft or robbery and associated offenses. Cut off from his drug, he passes through a period of dire suffering but at length may emerge detoxified. It is then that he most needs support, protection, care, and some kind of a job. But these needs have seldom been filled, and as a result he reverts to his old habits and associations.

Only very recently has this problem been given any thorough consideration and study. Some significant experiments are being made. There is increasing realization that addiction in itself should not be regarded as a matter for penal action, but as one for therapeutic measures. There are signs of progress, but the strategy of treatment is still somewhat controversial and the record of success has been low.

Two approaches are being explored and the prospects of real advancement are promising, especially when the two are combined. One is the establishment of rehabilitation centers with intensified supervision, constant experimentation, and background research. A good example is the California Rehabilitation Center. Most of the addicts are there under a law prescribing civil commitment, since the addiction takes such hold that they would not remain through the treatment except under compulsion. The program has met with some success, with fewer than the average number of relapses. It is significant that 80 per cent of the men under treatment had started the narcotic habit before the age of twenty. A newer program is that of Daytop Lodge, under the probation department of the Supreme Court of New York State, a "halfway house" for addicted probationers, in a beautiful setting at the opposite pole from the prison environment. Testing procedures are being developed and applied and the rehabilitative potentialities of therapy programs explored. Another and apparently quite remarkable experiment is the institution of Synanon at Santa Monica, California, which maintains a sort of tribal society for addicts, a system made possible by the strong *pater-familias* quality of its founder, Chuck Dederich. The evidence suggests that within the society a healthy drug-free spirit prevails. As with the other experiments mentioned, a longer period of exposure to the conditions of the outside world is needed before the degree of success achieved can be evaluated.

The second approach is through experimentation with drugs that may counteract the craving for heroin. Here quite important results have already been registered, especially with methadone, which seems to defeat the narcotic urge. Even if the substitute becomes habit-forming, the new habit appears from investigations thus far to be much less deleterious, costly, and dangerous than the old one.

While there is thus more promise than before for the rescue of the addict from his imperative craving, the way out of the deep cave of addiction is still hazardous and hard and long. Here as elsewhere primary stress must be laid on preventive measures. The insidious danger of the narcotic drug should be presented as realistically as possible. Attempts to prevent the use of narcotics by stopping the illegal traffic have in large measure been defeated by the ease of concealment and the great profits reaped by the gangsters who control the illicit market.

Concluding Observations on Strategy

As we review the variety of treatment programs now being developed in various parts of the country we are impressed by the manner in which modern developments in sociology, child psychology, psychoanalysis, and medical science are beginning to be reflected in them. Let us consider some of these developments and their relation to the more significant advances in the treatment procedure.

In the first place, good authorities have long held, and are more clearly demonstrating, through recent studies[10] that the earliest years of the child's upbringing within the family are the most crucial for the development alike of his morale and his potential IQ. Where the family sustains the child's basic trust, giving him self-confidence and self-reliance as well as the assurance of unity with the only society he knows, the chances are good that he will win through to success. An opposite picture is that of a child deprived of cultural advantages, brought up in demeaning squalor, perhaps as a member of a race subjected to gross discrimination and denied the opportunities other groups possess. Under such conditions the chances are that a sense of inferiority will destroy trust, numb aspiration, and stultify effort.

Obviously, then, what is done for and to the child at this very early stage will have a deeper affect on him than later treatment is likely to have. The lesson is particularly important both for the formation of his attitudes and the arresting of dangerous tendencies. Prevention is much easier, as well as much better, than cure. This lesson is still insufficiently heeded, but there are some signs of its being recognized. Henry Street Settlement, on New York City's Lower East Side, set up a pre-delinquent gang project designed to detect early symptoms of gang behavior in younger groups, which worked with them and their parents to wean them away from the influence of the older gangs.[11] The Settlement believes that through its intensive efforts it has helped uncommitted peer groups to achieve status in socially acceptable ways and has enabled parents to take a more enlightened interest in their children and thus to acquire more influence with them. The five groups in this after-school program ranged in age from eight to thirteen. Another project of similar character, a pre-teenage delinquency prevention program, is conducted under the auspices of the United Neighborhood Houses of New York City, the program being operated by nine member institutions situated in high-delinquency areas.[12] We need programs of a constructive preventive nature ranging all the way down to the nursery school.

Another established finding of sociological and sociopsychological research is that the majority of delinquent acts involve the participation or the influence of the youthful group, whether or not it takes the form of an established gang. This conclusion has been in evidence since the earlier studies of Breckenridge and Abbott, Healy and Bronner, Thrasher, Shaw, and various others. The presence of the group tends to neutralize internal conflicts, to lessen the embarrassment of a sense of guilt. It provides an alternative bond of security and belongingness when the youth finds himself at odds with the authoritative society. At the same time it becomes a barrier against influences brought to bear on him for his reform or rehabilitation.

Consequently there is a growing tendency to make the group the unit of treatment or therapy. We saw how in the Provo and Highfields experiments group guidance was primary and it has been prominent in the treatment systems we have described in the present chapter. It has also been extended to programs for parolees. In the difficult task of dealing with gang members it has proved the only effective method. The worker must make himself welcome within the relative intimacy of the gang, participant and helpful in its legitimate activities. Only by being accepted can he hope to redirect its more dangerous tendencies; only so is he likely to influence the attitudes of its individual members. This has been the experience of the New York City Youth Board and of the California Youth Authority. In his work with gangs in Boston, Miller found that while an effective worker will succeed in reducing the illegal operations of the gang, violations begin to increase after the announcement of his impending departure. One impediment to success is that a worker usually remains with a particular gang for only two or three years, and consequently can achieve only a limited redirection of the gang's interests and activities.

The importance of dealing with people in the total setting in which they function may be illustrated from another mode of treatment, distinguished as "milieu" therapy.[13] A continuity of specially adapted service within a particular environment is provided for a group of which the members exhibit some serious ailment, physical deficiency, or mental imbalance. The setting permits relatively free expression of antisocial or otherwise undesirable traits. The youth is confronted steadily and gently with the meaning and consequences of his behavior, as a means of assisting him to overcome these tendencies and to develop in time some behavior skills. Particularly significant applications of this method have been developed by Fritz Redl and his colleagues, by the Orthogenic School of Chicago, and by the McCords in their work at Wiltwyck Residential Center.[14] These have demonstrated that a rewarding degree of success can be achieved with groups of psychopathic youth, a category that had previously been regarded as beyond the scope of treatment.

Summation

1. The development of a considerable number of treatment programs under which a concerted effort is made to understand and deal with youth troubles in their relation to life conditions, family relationships, and other associations is definitely an advance in dealing with problems of delinquency.

2. In this development some progress has been made in the diagnosis of delinquency types and the screening of cases for differential treatment.

3. There is still rather frequently a lack or inadequacy of provision for the testing of progress as the work proceeds, and particularly for follow-up research to assess over two or three years at least the behavior of those who have been under treatment by comparison with that of an appropriate control group. This is still the most serious lack in the whole field of research on delinquency prevention and control.

4. The success of a treatment program depends primarily on the quality of the service. It calls not only for a variety of

cooperative professional skills but also for considerable experience, patient devotion, and fine discretion. For so important an objective no consideration of finance, proximity, or associations should be allowed to interfere with the endeavor to obtain the ablest available personnel.

The Over-all Planning of Anti-Delinquency Programs

As the volume of delinquency has increased, more services have been and are being provided for its control and prevention. These services have grown up sporadically and more or less independently. They are spread out over numerous agencies, public and private, and the public ones are distributed over several main city departments, while the states and the federal government are also actively concerned. On every level of service the question of integrated planning arises. The problem is complex and the need for some kind of coordination is imperative. In an earlier chapter we pointed out how any given service is more effective when it is linked up with other services and may be wholly negated unless it is supported by these other services. The lack of integrated planning means discontinuity and the dissipation of energies and funds.

Let us look more specifically at the need and the problem. A disturbed youth may be put under good guidance but unless something is done at the same time to change his relationship with his family and his family's relationship with him, the value of the guidance may be lost altogether. A youth may learn to form good habits in a custodial school for delinquents, but if he is not provided with after-care in the form of protection, temporary assistance, and help in finding a job, the benefit may be purely transitory. Delinquency is the result of the accumulation of unfavorable conditions, and if treatment is limited to one or more of these conditions, the others may balk its efficacy.

Similar conditions apply to the series of stages through which a youth proceeds when a charge of delinquency is brought against him. The case may go first to the police, to be followed by detention and then, after the adjudication of the court, he may be put on probation. At every stage, some screening and diagnosis are necessary but there may be no consistency in the process. The police screening decides whether the youngster is warned, referred to some welfare agency, or arrested. The court screening decides whether he is dismissed, discharged, put on probation, or sent to an institution. Are the police sufficiently trained, sufficiently in touch with the procedures of the court, to decide whether a case should be brought before the court? Does the judge know enough about the case to make the best decision for the welfare of the youth and is he sufficiently in touch with the nature of the institution to which he may commit the youth? Obviously, a close relationship between these stages of service is eminently desirable.

If this statement holds for the treatment process, it is certainly no less valid for the prevention of delinquency. Delinquency cannot be effectively prevented if attention is centered solely on children who already show delinquent tendencies, important as it is to deal with these. An effective system for the prevention of delinquency should be available to all children and will be no less valuable for those who have no delinquency taint than for those who have. In its functioning the school has a large part to play, but so has the family, the church, and all the other agencies attempting to provide opportunities for youth. Again, children who are particularly vulnerable or who are already showing signs of delinquent tendencies should be a concern of the neighborhood as a whole, and the neighborhood should be organized under professional leadership to discover such children, with the aid of the schools and welfare associations; otherwise they are likely to be neglected and uncared for until it is too late to arrest the formation of delinquent habits.

In light of these considerations, let us look at the problem of coordination as it affects the great city. We shall take New York City as our main illustration, since we have had occasion to give it special study. Like all great cities, it has a number of departments offering particular services for the young—the departments that deal with health, mental health, welfare, recreation, and correction. It has various agencies concerned with housing, urban renewal, foster care, day centers; its Board of Education has provided and developed a multitude of services for guidance—social, educational, and vocational.

The Youth Board is the city's major agency for anti-delinquency planning and the coordination of services, but for various reasons it has usually understood the function of coordination in an extremely limited sense. This board also has two other functions: contracting special services to private agencies concerned with the welfare of children in trouble, and an operating service concerned with street clubs for work with gangs, multi-problem families, and other activities.

While the Youth Board has contributed some important advances in particular areas and has itself filled some gaps in the city's operative services, it has never undertaken the major task of supervision and presumably was not expected to do so. Instead, it has established a rather loose liaison with various departments of the city and on the whole has been more concerned with the fulfillment of its other functions. It did not possess the status required to undertake full-scale coordination. In any event, whether the broad planning and integrating of closely related services should be conjoined with other functions is questionable.

A further problem has been that other bodies are also engaged in planning operations. The City Administrator's Office has had the special function of surveying and making reports on the efficacy and the interrelation of particular services. The Department of Welfare, in its turn, has been active in the expansion of a variety of services for health and social betterment. Again, the Community Council of Greater New York has been active in the consideration of a wide variety of city services, and its Regional and Neighborhood Planning Board has been concerned with the promotion of coherent local and regional associations. The Council, which has an elaborate structure, represents the major voluntary agencies of the City, with members of some City departments on it. Typically, in modern cities, a plethora of agencies arise to meet growing demands but little consideration is given to assuring that they will work together effectively.

The need for some kind of over-all supervision is further indicated by what has been happening to the two major enterprises recently set up within the city to provide all-around opportunities and services for the greatly disadvantaged youth of the city regions in which the projects are located. We refer to Haryou-Act and Mobilization for Youth. Such organizations should have ample freedom to devise their own plans for the exploration of the needs of the people they serve, to encourage these people to express in their own way their grievances and complaints, and to stimulate them to develop self-help while they are being ministered to by the workers for the projects. But such projects are liable to rouse objections from particular interest groups, political or economic. Moreover, they receive considerable financial contributions from both public and private sources and may be challenged to justify the way these funds are used. If they were under the aegis of a broad-based supervisory authority, they would possess a degree of security they otherwise lack. It is not unreasonable to suppose that if the two programs in question had been under the guardianship of a fully competent top-level unit responsible for the supervision and coordination of youth services, they would have been protected against unfair attacks and at the same time would be in less danger of giving grounds for such attacks. The kind of supervisory unit we have in mind would not interfere with the programs and policies of any responsible enterprise, but would make sure that it worked in proper relationship with sponsors, supporters, and city authorities.

The type of planning unit would vary with conditions but certain considerations are essential. The unit should be composed of persons of recognized standing and wide experience in endeavor to see that they are given full opportunity to establish the area of youth welfare, including persons who have shown high capacity in administration, citizens recognized for their broad and generous outlook, and one or two leading scholars. It would not carry on any direct operations of its own in the delinquency field, but would be full time devoted solely to over-all planning and supervision. It would enter into negotiations with the city's various agencies to develop policies to bridge the gap that so often exists between more or less autonomous city agencies. It would promote standards of service and would see that the conditions of service are such as to attract properly qualified personnel.

The planning unit, if it is to be effective, must be placed at a high level of government, say, within the Mayor's executive office. It would not undertake to control individual agencies but would use its influential position to assure their cooperation.

Such a planning unit should have attached to it a research group which would be in direct touch with the programs and operations of the various agencies in order to make recommendations for any necessary improvements, and also keep abreast of the studies being made in the field and bring to the attention of the planning unit any findings that might have a bearing on programs.

In the light of experience and research, the planning unit would seek to establish priorities and to promote policies that would bring them into effect. To give an illustration, a much neglected aspect of our present services is the failure to concentrate on *directed* prevention. By that, we mean those services that discover and give timely guidance and aid to those young persons who are beginning to fall into delinquent ways and who are particularly vulnerable because of their family situation or the tendency to truancy. At this early stage, the chances of rescuing such children are much greater than they are when habits of delinquency have been formed and confirmed.

Finally, the planning unit would take cognizance of the manifold services being rendered by voluntary agencies and would effect cooperation with official agencies.

While the need for the integration of programs may be greatest in the big city, with its multitude of agencies, public and private, it is also important in the state. On the state level, there is often a commission on crime and delinquency, or a council of community services, which has some general supervisory responsibilities. Some states—California and Minnesota, for example—have adopted the youth authority approach as a means of centralizing certain functions of delinquency control and treatment. The mechanisms for coordinating delinquency services vary greatly from state to state. In most states, however, there remains a considerable need for the more effective integration of state, regional, and municipal service.

Finally, on all levels of government, from federal to local, resources and programs are being provided to cope with the problems of youthful delinquency. The federal government has been greatly expanding its services to this end, especially since the establishment in 1961 of the President's Committee on Juvenile Delinquency and Youth Crime. In the same year, Congress passed its Juvenile Delinquency and Youth Offenses Control Act. Following up these initiatives, there are now important federal groups for training programs, special educational programs, many-sided programs for youth employment, and the recently established broad-based antipoverty campaign. The Department of Health, Education, and Welfare, along with its Health Institutes, has been active in furthering these developments.

These programs give new resources for states and localities, and this means an expansion of youth services all down the line. They call also for a redesigning of earlier services and for new liaisons between federal and state and between state and local activities in the field. To give fuller effectiveness to these new resources and opportunities, to avoid waste and overlapping and inefficiency, over-all planning is more imperative than ever before, both to assure the linkage between the different levels of public authority and to establish coherence and unity of effort within the operative programs of city and state alike.

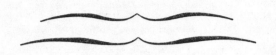

Notes

Chapter 1

1. As reported by the British Home Secretary, January 1963.
2. The figures for the various European countries are taken from the United Nations Bulletin, *New Forms of Juvenile Delinquency . . . ,* August 1960.
3. R. Perlman, "Delinquency Prevention: The Size of the Problem," (Washington, D.C.: U.S. Department of Health, Education, and Welfare), 1960.
4. The inadequacies of screening and the imperfections of diagnosis contribute to the lack of accuracy characteristic of delinquency statistics. We must never assume that official statistics in this area are at best more than rough approximations. One particularly serious defect is the unknown relationship between detected and undetected delinquencies, which probably is highly variable under different conditions and in different areas. For an able and learned discussion of this and other problems of delinquency statistics, see Isidor Chein, *Some Epidemiological Vectors of Delinquency and its Control* (New York University: Research Center for Human Relations), 1963.

Chapter 2

1. Sheldon and Eleanor T. Glueck, *Unraveling Juvenile Delinquency* (Cambridge, Mass.: Harvard), 1950, and other works.
2. Among studies that bear out this conclusion we may cite Robert J. Havighurst and Hilda Tobin, *Adolescent Character and Personality* (New York: Wiley), 1963, and Margaret Mead, *And Keep Your Powder Dry* (New York: Morrow), 1965.
3. Albert J. Reiss, Jr., and Albert L. Rhodes, "Delinquency and Social Class Structure," *American Sociological Review,* October 1961.
4. Final Report No. 2, 1961.
5. Study presented as a dissertation for the Ph.D. degree at Columbia University. It was written under the direction of the present writer.
6. "A Five Year Study of Early School-Leavers," *Guidance News,* NYC Board of Education, March 1957.

7. "Students and Their Progress in the '600' Day Schools," NYC Juvenile Delinquency Evaluation Project, Report No. 6.
8. *Cf.* W. C. Kvaraceus, *Juvenile Delinquency and the Schools* (Yonkers, N.Y.), 1954; Lane and Witty, "The Educational Attainment of Delinquent Boys," *Journal of Educational Psychology,* Vol. 25, 1934.
9. Miller, Margolin, and Yolles, "Epidemiology of Reading Disabilities," *American Journal of Public Health,* Vol. 47, 1957.

Chapter 3

1. William Healy and Augusta F. Bronner, *New Light on Delinquency and Its Treatment* (New Haven: Yale), 1936.
2. Fritz Redl and David Wineman, *Children Who Hate* (New York: The Free Press), 1951.
3. William and Joan McCord, *Psychopathy and Delinquency* (New York: Grune & Stratton), 1956.

Chapter 4

1. William Healy and Augusta F. Bronner, *Delinquents and Criminals* (New York), 1926.
2. See especially E. Greenwood, "New Directions in Delinquency Research, a Commentary on a Study by Bernard Lander," *The Social Service Review,* Vol. 30, June 1956; also David J. Bordua, "Juvenile Delinquency and Anomie, an Attempt at Replication," *Social Problems,* Vol. 6, Winter 1958–1959.

Chapter 5

1. C. R. Shaw and H. D. McKay, *Juvenile Delinquency and Urban Areas* (Chicago: University of Chicago Press), 1942.
2. William L. Warner and Paul S. Lunt, *Yankee City Series* (New Haven: Yale University Press), 1941, Chapter 6.
3. Milton Barron, *The Juvenile in Delinquent Society* (New York: Knopf), 1954.
4. Albert K. Cohen, *Delinquent Boys: The Structure of the Gang* (New York: The Free Press), 1955.
5. Walter B. Miller, "Lower Class Culture as a Generating Medium of Gang Delinquency," *Journal of Social Issues,* No. 3, 1958.
6. Richard A. Cloward and Lloyd E. Ohlin, *New Perspectives on Juvenile Delinquency* (New York: New York School of Social Work), 1959.
7. Robert K. Merton, *Social Theory and Social Structure* (New York: The Free Press), 1957.
8. Albert J. Reiss and Albert L. Rhodes, "Delinquency and Social Class Structure," *American Sociological Review,* October 1961; Robert Dubois, "Deviant Behavior and Social Structure," *American Sociological Review,* April 1959; John I. Kitsuse and David C. Dietrick,

"Delinquent Boys, A Critique," *ibid*. For a broad-based review of the whole issue see Herbert A. Bloch and Gilbert Geis, *Man, Crime and Society* (New York: Random House), 1961, pp. 433–441; Herbert A. Bloch and Frank T. Flynn, *Delinquency* (New York: Random House), 1956, Chapter 8.

9. The detailed statistics are presented in New York City Juvenile Delinquency Evaluation Project, Final Report No. 2, *Delinquency in the Great City*, 1961, directed by the writer.
10. Reiss and Rhodes, *op. cit.*

Chapter 6

1. Walter B. Miller, *Social Service Review*, Vol. 33, No. 3, 1959.
2. F. Ivan Nye, James F. Short, Jr., and Virgil J. Olson, "Socioeconomic Status and Delinquent Behavior," *American Journal of Sociology*, Vol. 63, January 1958.

Chapter 7

1. For a brief account of the Mexican system, see A. H. Maslow and R. Diaz-Guerrero, "Adolescence and Juvenile Delinquency in Two Different Cultures," *Festschrift for Gardner Murphy*, Peatman and Hartley, eds. (New York), 1960.
2. J. D. Lohman, "Juvenile Delinquency, Its Dimensions, Its Conditions, Techniques of Control, Proposals for Action," *Juvenile Delinquency Prevention and Control*. Hearings before the Subcommittee on Juvenile Delinquency, U.S. Senate, 86th Congress, First Session, 1959, National Institute of Mental Health, 1960.
3. See, for example, W. C. Kvaraceus, *Juvenile Delinquency and the Schools* (Yonkers, N.Y.), 1954.
4. Albert K. Cohen, *Delinquent Boys: The Culture of the Gang* (New York: The Free Press), 1955, pp. 13, 14.
5. *Ibid.*, p. 150.
6. *Ibid.*, p. 153.
7. Lloyd E. Ohlin and William C. Lawrence, "Social Interaction among Clients as a Treatment Problem," *Social Work*, IV, 1959, pp. 3–13.
8. Ruth Tefferteller, "Delinquency Prevention Through Revitalizing Parent-Child Relationships," *Annals, American Academy of Political and Social Science*, 322, 1959, pp. 69–78; M. Gold and J. A. Winter, *Children, Youth and Family Life* (Ann Arbor: Institute for Social Research, University of Michigan), October 1961.
9. Arthur Hillman, *Neighborhood Centers Today*, National Federation of Settlements, New York, 1960, 239 pp.
10. Melvin Herman, "The Work Group as an Instrument in Enhancing the Employability of Youth," Mobilization for Youth, presented at the National Conference on Social Welfare, Cleveland, Ohio, May 23, 1963 (for staff only).
11. *Ibid.*
12. Lawrence R. Ephron and Irving Piliavin, *A New Approach to Juvenile Delinquency*. A Study of the Youth for Service Program in

San Francisco, Survey Research Center, University of California, Berkeley, California.

Chapter 8

1. Milton Barron, *The Juvenile in Delinquent Society* (New York: Knopf), 1954.
2. Henry Robert Goddard, *The Kallikak Family* (New York: Macmillan), 1919, Chapter 9; Richard Dugdale, *The Jukes* (New York: Putnam), 1877, Chapter 9.

Chapter 9

1. Herbert A. Bloch, "The Inadequacies of Research in Delinquency Causation," *National Probation and Parole Association Journal,* Vol. 1, July 1955.

Chapter 11

1. Frank Reissman, *The Culturally Deprived Child* (New York: Harper & Row), 1962.
2. *The Demonstration Guidance Project: 1957–1962 Pilot Program for Higher Horizons,* Board of Education of the City of New York.
3. Charlotte D. Elmott, Jane Criner, and Ralph Wagner, *The Troublesome Ten Per Cent, A Report of a Demonstration of School Social Work,* Santa Barbara City Schools, Santa Barbara, California, 1961; *Review of the Role of the Schools in Mental Health,* United Federation of Teachers, New York City, December 1963, p. 5.
4. Donald Cook and Seymour Rubenfeld, "Settings and Causes of Juvenile Delinquency," Chapter III, *An Assessment of Current Mental Health and Social Science Knowledge,* Appendix II, National Institute of Mental Health, February 1960, p. 15.
5. Terry Ferrer, "Classroom Revolution," *New York Herald Tribune* 1963 (reprint).
6. Bryce Perkins, "Team Teaching, Current Developments in Education," *Educational Perspectives,* February 1962 (reprint).
7. *Norwalk School Improvement Program,* April 1962–August 1963, Norwalk Board of Education, Norwalk, Conn.
8. Jacob Landers, *Higher Horizons Progress Report,* Board of Education of the City of New York, January 1963.
9. Adele Franklin, "The All-Day Neighborhood Services," *Annals of the American Academy of Political and Social Science,* vol. 322, 1959, pp. 62–68; *The All-Day Neighborhood Schools,* Interim Report XIII, Juvenile Delinquency Evaluation Project of the City of New York, December 1959.
10. *A Cooperative Study for the Better Utilization of Teacher Competencies,* Final Report, Central Michigan College, Mt. Pleasant, Michigan, 1960.
11. James B. Conant, *Education of American Teachers* (New York: McGraw-Hill), 1963.

12. *Students and Their Programs in the "600" Day Schools,* Interim Report VI, Juvenile Delinquency Evaluation Project of the City of New York, December 1959, pp. 7, 8.
13. Gordon P. Liddle, "Relationship of Reading and Delinquency: Role of the School in the Prevention of Delinquency," *Cooperative Research Monograph #10,* p. 50.
14. *Ibid.,* p. 55.
15. *Ibid.,* p. 58.
16. Daniel Schrieber, "Juvenile Delinquency and the School Drop-Out Problem," *Federal Probation,* September 1963, p. 17.
17. *Ibid.,* p. 18.
18. *Annual Report 1962–1963,* Division of Child Welfare, Bureau of Educational and Vocational Guidance, Board of Education of the City of New York, pp. 21–28.
19. *Ibid.,* pp. 28–33.
20. *Ibid.,* pp. 86–88.
21. George T. Donahue and Sol Nitchtern, "A School District Program for Identification and Adaptation to the Needs of Anxiously Disturbed Children."
22. Nathan Glazer, "Out of School, Out of Work," No. 42, July 18, 1963.
23. Tom Wicker, "10,000 Will Return to School After U.S. Drop-Out Campaign," *The New York Times,* Monday, September 19, 1963.
24. *Reducing the School Drop-Out Rate—A Report on the Holding Power Project,* The University of the State of New York, State Education Department, Bureau of Guidance, Albany, 1963.
25. *Annual Report,* Division of Child Welfare, *op. cit.,* p. 38.
26. *Ibid.,* pp. 76–78.
27. *Project: School Drop-outs,* National Education Association, Vol. II, No. 1, September 1963, pp. 2–6 passim.
28. Harold J. Dillon, *Work Experience in Secondary Schools,* National Child Labor Committee, June 1946, pp. 89–92.
29. *Delinquency Prevention through Guidance in the Schools,* Final Report No. 3, Juvenile Delinquency Evaluation Project of the City of New York, August 1961.

Chapter 12

1. Donald Cook and Seymour Rubenfeld, "Prevention and Treatment in the Community," Chapter VII, *An Assessment of Current Mental Health and Social Science Knowledge Concerning Juvenile Delinquency,* February 1960, p. 3.
2. Martin Gold and Jay Allan Winter, *A Selective Review of Community-Based Programs for Preventing Delinquency,* Institute of Social Research, University of Michigan, Ann Arbor, Michigan, October 1961, pp. 160, 161.
3. *Jobless Youth: A Challenge to Community Organization,* National Social Welfare Assembly, June 1963, p. 9.
4. *Opening Opportunities: New Haven's Comprehensive Program for Community Progress,* New Haven Youth Development Program, April 1962, p. 2; *New Haven Youth Development Program, Part 2,* Community Progress, Inc., New Haven, Connecticut, October 1963,

p. 7; Max Doverman, *New Haven Youth Development Program: Its Contents, Structure and Future Implications.* A Report to the Project's Planning Committee. Community Council of Greater New Haven, October 28, 1963.

5. *Progress Report:* Joint Youth Development Committee, Chicago, Illinois, February 8, 1964; *Gateways for Youth,* A proposal by the St. Louis Human Development Corporation, St. Louis, Missouri, January 8, 1964; *The Boston Program,* Action for Boston Community Development, Inc., Boston, Massachusetts, September 9, 1964, 9 pp.; *Boston Youth Opportunities Program,* Action for Boston Community Development, Inc., Boston, Massachusetts, December 1963, pp. 209, 210.

6. *The All-Day Neighborhood Schools,* Interim Report XIII, Juvenile Delinquency Evaluation Project of the City of New York, December 1959; Adele, Franklin, "The All-Day Neighborhood Services," *Annals of the American Academy of Political and Social Science,* Vol. 322, 1959, pp. 62–68; *The Demonstration Guidance Project: 1957–1962 Pilot Program for Higher Horizons,* Board of Education of the City of New York.

7. *The Chicago Demonstration on Delinquency Control and Prevention, Intentions and Directions,* a summary statement on the Joint Youth Development Committee's Proposal, November 12, 1962, mimeographed statement #630, pp. 4–7.

8. *Gateways for Youth, op. cit.,* pp. 95, 96.

9. *Youth in the Ghetto,* A study of the consequences and a blueprint for change, Harlem Youth Opportunities Unlimited, New York City, 1964.

10. *Action on the Lower East Side,* Progress Report and Proposal, Mobilization for Youth, New York City, July 1962–June 1964.

11. "A Proposal for the Prevention and Control of Delinquency by Expanding Opportunities," Mobilization for Youth, New York City, 1961.

Chapter 13

1. Jean Selvidge, "The Police Juvenile Bureau's Job," *National Probation Parole Association Journal,* vol. III, no. 1, January 1957, pp. 41–44.

2. Alfred J. Kahn, *Planning Community Services for Children in Trouble* (New York: Columbia University Press), 1963, p. 224.

3. G. A. Mitchell, "The Youth Bureau: A Sociological Study," unpublished Master's thesis, Wayne State University, Detroit, Michigan, 1957.

4. Clyde B. Vedder, *The Juvenile Offender* (Garden City, N.Y.: Doubleday), 1954, p. 193.

5. Saul Bernstein, *Youth on the Streets* (New York: Association Press), 1964, pp. 71–73.

6. Tom V. Waldron, Police-School Liaison Program, Flint, Michigan Police Department, 1962, 42 pp.

7. *Planning Community Services . . . , op. cit.,* p. 24.

8. *The Police Department,* Interim Report No. 11, Juvenile Delinquency

Evaluation Project of the City of New York, December 1956, Table III, p. VI.

Chapter 14

1. Paul W. Alexander, "Constitutional Rights in Juvenile Court," in *Justice for the Child,* Margaret K. Rosenheim (New York: The Free Press), 1962, p. 92.
2. Elliot Studt, "The Client's Image," in *Justice for the Child, op. cit.,* pp. 206–207.
3. Alfred J. Kahn, "Court and Community," in *Justice for the Child, op. cit.,* pp. 228–229.
4. Sophie M. Robison, *Juvenile Delinquency, Its Nature and Control* (New York: Holt), 1960, p. 334.
5. Howard E. Fradkin, "Dispositions and Dilemmas of American Juvenile Courts," in *Justice for the Child, op. cit.,* pp. 136–137.
6. Negley K. Teeters and John O. Reinemann, *The Challenge of Delinquency* (New York: Prentice-Hall), 1950, pp. 377–378.
7. Harris B. Peck, *et al., A New Pattern for Mental Health Services in Children's Court* (Springfield, Ill.: Charles C Thomas), 1938, pp. 44, 48.
8. Justine W. Polier, *A View from the Bench,* National Council on Crime and Delinquency, New York City, 1964, pp. 8–9.
9. Mary H. Speed, "A Guidance Clinic for Probation," *California Youth Authority Quarterly,* Winter 1961, pp. 30–32.

Chapter 15

1. Robert Schulman, *This Year in Our Training Schools,* address given at the Second Annual Conference of New York State Training Schools, New Paltz, New York, September 9, 1963.
2. Alfred J. Kahn, *Planning Community Services for Children in Trouble* (New York: Columbia University Press), 1963.
3. Ruth Shonle Cavan, *Juvenile Delinquency, Development, Treatment and Control* (New York: Lippincott), 1962, p. 305.
4. Juvenile Delinquency Evaluation Project, City of New York, *Three Residential Treatment Centers,* New York, 1958.
5. Joseph H. Louchheim, *The Delinquency Problem and Approaches to Its Solution, as Seen from the Standpoint of the Institutions,* November 17, 1958.
6. Juvenile Delinquency Evaluation Project, City of New York, *The Institutionalization of Young Delinquents,* Report No. XI, p. 6, 1958.
7. Clarke, Freeman, and Trent, unpublished report on Warwick Training School.
8. Seymour Rubenfeld, "The Inmate Culture in the Correctional Institute for Mental Health, in Support of Report to the Congress on Juvenile Delinquency," Appendix II, February 1960, Chapter V, pp. 9, 16–20.
9. Howard W. Polsky, *Cottage Six: The Social System of Delinquent Boys in Residential Treatment* (New York: Russell Sage Foundation), 1962, pp. 168–182.

10. Herbert A. Bloch and Frank T. Flynn, *Delinquency: The Juvenile Offender in America Today* (New York: Random House), 1956, p. 453.
11. John W. Mannering, mimeographed memorandum, Department of Public Welfare, Wisconsin, 1957, in *Berkshire Farm Monographs,* December 1962.
12. *Berkshire Farm Monographs,* December 1962, Vol. I, No. 1, p. 19.
13. The Children's Village, Dobbs Ferry, New York, Policies and Procedures, *Handbook for Orientation Seminar,* Fall 1962, pp. 22–25.
14. Rosemary P. Peters, "Treatment Needs of Juvenile Offenders," California State Board of Corrections, Monograph #1, July 1960.
15. North Carolina Board of Corrections and Training, "Second Annual Proceedings Workshop for Cottage Counselors," February 5–7, 1963.
16. Albert Elias, "Highfields After Five Years," *The Welfare Reporter, New Jersey Institutions and Agencies,* Trenton, N.J., January 1958, pp. 3–17; Albert Elias and Jerome Rabow, "Post-Release Adjustment of Highfields Boys, 1955–57," *The Welfare Reporter, New Jersey Institutions and Agencies,* Trenton, N.J., January 1960, pp. 7–12; H. Ashley Weeks, *Youthful Offenders at Highfields* (Ann Arbor: University of Michigan), 1963, p. 49; *General Statement 1964–65 and Annual Report 1962–63,* Highfields Residential Group Center, Hopewell, N.J.
17. H. Ashley Weeks, *op. cit.,* p. 146.
18. Lamar T. Empey and Jerome Rabow, "The Provo Experiment in Delinquency Rehabilitation," *American Sociological Review,* vol. 26, no. 5, October 1961.
19. Robert Schulman, "The Group Residence—Part of a Network of Rehabilitative Services," address delivered at the New York State Welfare Conference, New York City, November 27, 1962, pp. 5–6.

Chapter 16

1. Donald C. Cook, "Some Evaluative Studies," in *An Assessment of Current Mental Health and Social Science Knowledge Concerning Juvenile Delinquency,* Appendix II, Chapter VI, February 1960, pp. 31, 32.
2. Donald C. Cook and Seymour Rubenfeld, "Settings and Causes of Delinquency," Chapter III, p. 45, and "Some Evaluative Studies," Chapter VI, p. 25, in *An Assessment of Current Mental Health and Social Science Knowledge Concerning Juvenile Delinquency,* Appendix II, February 1960; *Reaching the Unreached,* Monograph #5, New York City Youth Board, 1958.
3. R. C. Wirt and P. F. Briggs, Personality and Environmental Factors in the Development of Delinquency (unpublished manuscript), University of Minnesota, quoted in Donald C. Cook, "Settings and Causes of Delinquency," *op. cit.,* p. 76.
4. Joseph C. Lagey and Beverly Ayres, *Community Treatment Programs for Multi-Problem Families,* a survey of 260 North American Communities Community Chest and Councils of the Greater Vancouver Area, December 1962, pp. 2–8 passim.

5. *Hyde Park Project,* Welfare Council of Metropolitan Chicago, Illinois, May 1955–1958, pp. 65–75.

6. Salvador Minuchin, Edgar Auerswald, Charles King, and Clara Rabinowitz, *The Study and Treatment of Families Who Produce Multiple Acting-out Boys,* Wiltwyck School for Boys, Inc., for presentation at the American Orthopsychiatric Association Convention, March 1963, pp. 2–13 (to be published); Edgar Auerswald, *Developmental Effects of Poverty on Children of Hard-Core Urban Families—Implications for Nosology and Treatment,* Wiltwyck School for Boys, Inc., for presentation at the American Orthopsychiatric Association Convention, March 1964, p. 16 (to be published); Charles H. King and Clara Rabinowitz, *The Impact of Familial Perceptions of Public Welfare Agency Practice on Family Attitudes with Special Reference to Delinquent Children,* Wiltwyck School for Boys, Inc., for presentation at the American Orthopsychiatric Association Convention, March 1964, pp. 11, 12.

7. *Community Treatment Project, First Year Report of Action and Evaluation,* Operation and Research Staff, Department of Youth Authority, Youth and Adult Corrections Agency, State of California, June 1, 1963; *An Evaluation of Community Treatment for Delinquents,* Community Treatment Project Reports #1 through 5, Operation and Research Staff, Department of Youth Authority, Youth and Adult Corrections Agency, State of California, August 1, 1962, pp. 9, 10.

8. *Ibid.,* pp. 21, 22.

9. *Ibid.,* pp. 25, 27.

10. Benjamin S. Bloom, *Stability and Change in Human Characteristics* (New York: Wiley), 1964.

11. Ruth S. Tefferteller, "Delinquency Prevention Through Revitalizing Parent-Child Relationships, *The Annals of the American Academy of Political and Social Science,* vol. 322, 1959, pp. 69–78.

12. Goodwin P. Garfield, United Neighborhood Houses Pre-Teen Delinquency Prevention Project (speech), Institute on Services to Multi-Problem Families, sponsored by the National Federation of Settlements Training Center, March 5–7, 1964.

13. J. H. Reid and H. R. Hagan, *Residential Treatment of Emotionally Disturbed Children;* a descriptive study, New York Child Welfare League, 1952, quoted in Donald C. Cook and Seymour Rubenfeld, "The Nature of Treatment," *op. cit.,* Chapter IV, p. 20.

14. William and Joan McCord, *Psychopathy and Delinquency* (New York: Grune & Stratton), 1956.

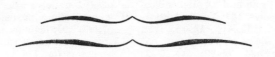

Index